"You will be changed as you read this book—a book of grief and comfort. Written without easy answers, but with gritty, courageous prayer, wrestling like Jacob with God's angel."

> —**Eugene H. Peterson**, Professor Emeritus of Spiritual Theology, Regent College, Vancouver, B.C.; translator of *The Message*

"*Getting Out of Bed in the Morning* is a safe place to reconcile painful losses—a graceful guide through the uncharted and often complex landscape of grief and loss. Alice's heart whispers an understanding that comes only from one who has tasted consuming heartache, yet uncovered the hope of God's sustaining grace."

> —**Jo Ann Fore**, author, founder of *WriteWhereItHurts.org*

"As I walk along my own journey through grief, there are many paths ahead of me that I could choose. Alice shares wisdom gained through her own heart's wrestle with God and gently encourages me onto a path that leads to healing, wholeness, and eternal hope."

> —**Elaine Howlett**, bereaved mom, grief educator and speaker, author of *Lazarus, Come Out!*

"Don't look for clichés or platitudes or easy answers in this book, but take solace in a companion and trustworthy guide who can help direct us fearlessly through the valley of the shadow of death. Wisler has the unique capacity to come alongside us in our seasons of darkness and to offer both the solidarity of a fellow sufferer, and the insistence that hope is reasonable, because God is still redeeming the brokenhearted."

> —**Eric E. Peterson**, pastor, Colbert Presbyterian Church, Colbert, Washington

"In *Getting Out of Bed in the Morning: Reflections of Comfort in Heartache*, Alice speaks to the heart from the heart! I found myself in many of the verses. Run, don't walk, and get this book. Peace and comfort are only a page away."

   —**Debby Stephenson**, founder/director of *Courageous Kidz—A Safe Haven for Kids with Cancer*

"Alice's new book brings a beautiful blend of practical steps with powerful messages from God's Word. Each stage of the book brings back the confidence that, indeed, we will wake up tomorrow—renewed and filled with God's grace—so the day will shine with a new peace and a sweet kind of joy."

   —**Janet Perez Eckles**, author of *Simply Salsa: Dancing Without Fear at God's Fiesta*

"Truly wonderful book. Practical, yet poignant. . . . Through her suggested prayers, insights, and walking exercises, Wisler guides the grieving soul to the Great Physician's healing."

   —**Linda Rondeau**, author of *The Other Side of Darkness*

"Alice Wisler has made a noble effort to put into devotional form a journey from deep sorrow, anger, and grief to one of trust and knowing God still loves you despite the tribulations of severe loss. Not everyone has lost a beloved child to disease, a car wreck, or murder, but those who have can connect with what Alice communicates in her new devotional, *Getting Up in the Morning.*"

   —**Dr. Linda B. Greer**, writer, blogger, bereaved mother

GETTING
Out of Bed
IN THE MORNING

REFLECTIONS OF COMFORT IN HEARTACHE

ALICE J. WISLER

LEAFWOOD
PUBLISHERS

GETTING OUT OF BED IN THE MORNING
Reflections of Comfort in Heartache

LEAFWOOD
P U B L I S H E R S

Copyright 2013 by Alice J. Wisler

ISBN 978-0-89112-419-1
LCCN 2012037284

Printed in the United States of America

ALL RIGHTS RESERVED
No part of this publication may be reproduced, stored in a retrieval system, or transmitted in any form by any means—electronic, mechanical, photocopying, or otherwise—without prior written consent.

Scripture quotations, unless otherwise noted, are from The Holy Bible, New International Version. Copyright 1984 and 2011, International Bible Society. Used by permission of Zondervan Publishers. Scripture quotations noted NLT are taken from the Holy Bible, *New Living Translation*, copyright 1996, 2004. Used by permission of Tyndale House Publishers, Inc., Wheaton, Illinois 60189. All rights reserved. Scripture quotations taken from *The Message*. Copyright 1993, 1994, 1995, 1996, 2000, 2001, 2002. Used by permission of NavPress Publishing Group.

Published in association with MacGregor Literary, 2373 N.W. 185th Avenue, Suite 165, Hillsboro, OR 97124.

LIBRARY OF CONGRESS CATALOGING-IN-PUBLICATION DATA
Wisler, Alice J.
  Getting out of bed in the morning : reflections of comfort in heartache / Alice J. Wisler.
    p. cm.
  ISBN 978-0-89112-419-1
  1. Loss (Psychology)--Religious aspects--Christianity--Meditations. 2. Consolation. I. Title.
  BV4909.W58 2013
  242'.4--dc23
                                                                    2012037284

Cover design by Marc Whitaker, ThinkPen Design
Interior text design by Sandy Armstrong

Leafwood Publishers is an imprint of
Abilene Christian University Press

1626 Campus Court | Abilene, Texas 79601
1-877-816-4455 | www.leafwoodpublishers.com

13 14 15 16 17 18 / 7 6 5 4 3 2 1

Hear my prayer, O LORD;
let my cry for help come to you.
Do not hide your face from me
when I am in distress.
Turn your ear to me;
when I call, answer me quickly.

—PSALM 102:1–2

To Daniel's siblings—
Rachel, Benjamin, and Elizabeth—
three of my best instructors.

TABLE OF CONTENTS

SECTION FOUR
Sustained to Thrive

SECTION FIVE
Sustained to Hope

ACKNOWLEDGMENTS

I owe much to many, including:

Paul Immanuel for his Sunday school class at Blacknall Memorial Presbyterian Church, The Compassionate Friends, Bereaved Parents of the USA, my agent Chip MacGregor, Leafwood Publishers for believing in this project, and those along the way who have been encouragers to me.

PREFACE

I set out to write a book about me—my anguish, my loss, my pain, my doubt, my questions. Instead I was pointed to God and wrote about His grace, His love, His faithfulness, and His forgiveness. Within those are His answers.

We often think it's all about us—how much we suffer, how much we cry, how tormented we feel. But when we weigh all of our misery against His grace, His grace outweighs it all. God's compassion is stronger, fiercer than our struggles, and His love more constant, radiant, and healing than any problem in our den of lions.

If you are early in your grief, you may not understand what I'm talking about. You might still be at odds with God, and while the title of this book caught your attention, as you flip through the pages, that's all you liked. That's okay. God meets us wherever we are and no amount of disbelief, anger, or frustration keeps Him from loving His children. It has taken me fifteen years, from the worst heartache of my life, to come to this place of comfort, this stream of beauty. And I never thought I'd be here. When my son first died, I told God that we would only communicate in passing, like a neighbor I don't like when I see her over the fence. I almost wished I had had no past with God—no history, no conversion story—so that I didn't have to be angry with Him for my loss. God would be distant from now on. As I learned to adapt to my heartache, I would not expect anything from Him again.

I am one who had to wrestle. Like Jacob, I did. I groaned and I fought and groaned some more. And through it all, I was surprised. What I thought I'd discarded for good, instead became a new song in my mouth. I welcomed a stronger, genuine, more realistic faith—a possession I keep within my broken heart, a gift no moth or thief can steal.

INTRODUCTION

I lie down and sleep;
I wake again, because the Lord sustains me.
—PSALM 3:5

*I*t all came about with a walk one summer day in August. Up until that day I was not an avid exerciser. The summer before, I'd attempted to get into some daily heart-healthy movement with morning walks around my neighborhood. I didn't particularly enjoy the rapid breathing or sweaty armpits, so I didn't continue and I wasn't bothered that I hadn't.

But for whatever reason—perhaps it was the actual sidewalk that runs up and down Pickett Road, shaded by trees on one side—after dropping my son off at work, I decided to walk. He was fifteen, this was his first job, and it was at the Structure House in Durham, which offered a weight loss program. As my son prepped food and waited on tables for those with eating issues, I walked along the smooth sidewalks and thought of my own issues.

My own circumstances were ones that, over the years, had marked me as a person: born and raised in Japan, I was a TCK (Third Culture Kid); at age thirty-six I buried my oldest son; then it was living with a bipolar spouse, divorce, single mom-hood, and remarriage. There were others, issues I didn't like to allude to and wanted to keep in the dark, like greed, jealously, and fear. When I finished my walk, I peeled off my Reeboks and felt proud that I had endured exercise.

The next day, I drove him to work in the afternoon and thought that if I did it yesterday, then by golly, I should try again today. Perhaps it was the allurement that there were still things to discover. So, I parked my Jeep and stepped out on the sidewalk feeling comradely with other joggers and walkers.

Walking provided me with a new way of thinking. I noticed that walking gave me some creative thoughts, and I always like to delve into creativity. I thought about endurance. And I would continue to think of it and of questions, perplexing and demanding, because that day was not my last day to walk. In fact, that week began my daily walking routine. I knew what I needed for my journey—my tennis shoes, my pink "I Love New Orleans" cap, my elastic-waist black pants from Target, and my "Happy Burro" T-shirt, a souvenir from a hole-in-the-wall eatery in Beatty, Nevada. My sunglasses were also essential; they hid the fact that I had no makeup on.

Getting into the habit of having a daily walking regime was not easy. I played with words like "change," "struggle," "how long," and "should I keep going?" My thoughts reminded me of Psalms, the book of the Bible we were studying in my Sunday school class. Those first days, I teetered, wondering whatever caused me to have a desire to walk, to try, and whether today could be my last day to attempt this sweaty and tedious task. Each day I wrote on my calendar when I walked. The first week I walked every day. The next week it was a bit harder to be faithful to this new calling; but after clocking my time and the distance I'd walked, I realized it really wasn't taking but thirty minutes of my day. Soon walking became a challenge I wanted to succeed in.

They say it takes thirty days to start a habit, and within thirty days, walking was the highlight of my afternoon. I increased my speed and added fifteen more minutes to my routine so that I was walking three miles each day. Sure, I liked the health benefits, and my backside even started to shrink. But what I really celebrated was what God taught me as I walked. God met me in my commitment. And, hence, I got to thinking about writing this book.

The start and commitment to my exercise was tough at first. So is getting out of bed in the morning when you are in the middle of dealing with a broken heart. You have to be willing and committed to achieve the task. No one can make you do it. You may ask, "How can I get moving and going to face the day's challenges when my eyes are weary from tears?" You want to know how long, why you have to struggle, and most importantly, where is God in all of this?

After you succeed in getting up the first day, then there is the next morning—when you feel just as bad—and the next, and trillions of mornings after that.

This collection of devotions is for those who cry out, "Why is my life so hard?!" Others seem to have it easy. Why is there so much pain? I'm in thick smog and can't seem to get out. Why can't I reach my goals? What is wrong with me? Where is hope?

This book is for anyone struggling. It is written for those like me—a sufferer of and a wrestler with heartache. Heartache comes in the form of the loss of a loved one, a career, health or finances, hopes and dreams, loss of marriage, loss of identity, and loss of relationships. These struggles present a multitude of questions to grapple with, and in these pages we'll talk about them. We'll talk about God, especially about how He sustains us so that we can carry on and even thrive.

My book is written in small reflections, offering a theme with thoughts to ponder, a Scripture verse or two (mainly from the psalms because they are such a great selection for both sorrow and praise), and a prayer. And it is my prayer that as we journey together and discover how God sustains us to continue in our relationship with Him, His mercy, love, grace, and peace will abide in our hearts.

And as we begin, I present you with the definition of a word which will be used throughout this book—a word which will bring focus to our journey.

Sustain:

- to support, hold, or bear up from below; bear the weight of, as a structure.
- to bear (a burden, charge, etc.).
- to undergo, experience, or suffer (injury, loss, etc.); endure without giving way or yielding.
- to keep (a person, the mind, the spirits, etc.) from giving way, as under trial or affliction.
- to keep up or keep going, as an action or process: to sustain a conversation.

—DICTIONARY.COM

SECTION ONE

Sustained to Weep

One

TEARS AS FOOD

*My tears have been my food
day and night . . .*
—PSALM 42:3

W hen my son died, my missionary mother said to me with tears and a large embrace, "Alice, you are called to suffer."

At the time, I wasn't exactly sure what this entailed. My eyes were red and puffy, and I'd already gone through a whole box of hospital tissues—the kind that stick to your face. Later, I would invest in tissues that don't bond to your nose and cheeks, decorating them with white specks.

Suffer! I hated that word. *Called*. Somehow, I added God to that word. All my life I'd heard about how God calls us. Jesus called the disciples to follow Him (Matt. 4:18–22), we are called to be set apart (1 Pet. 2:9). Why would anyone be called to suffer? I'd rather be called to win the lottery or called to a feast at the Washington and Duke, a prestigious inn and restaurant in my town of Durham, North Carolina.

Yearning daily for my son, I was a sea of raging emotions.

And the only one I could pour my feelings out to was my journal, given to me by a hospital nurse, a friend of my son's. So I wrote, and wrote some more. Part of me hoped that by writing, I would finally find a loophole in his death, and that would bring my son back to us.

Surely God made a mistake in letting him die. I thought it was extremely illogical for God not to have healed him from his cancer. Daniel was a cute kid, vivacious, and he loved Jesus the way four-year-olds do. In the hospital chapel, he'd lower his bald head and asked God to heal his "boo-boo." God seemed far from me during those days of early grief. I felt abandoned.

Looking back on the devastation of that new grief, I remember how tears were a huge part of my journey. Right now, they could be part of your daily lifestyle, too. We eat tears as food; we wake to tears and often cry ourselves to sleep. On one hand, tears are natural and a good cry can be healthy and healing. After all, God made tears. On the other hand, too many tears wear us down and give us headaches.

I hope that even in our distress we will remember that God sees our tears. He is not indifferent to our suffering. Nothing that happens to us eludes His eyes. We can pour out our longings to Him as we would to a friend. Even if we feel abandoned, removed, at odds with Him, He listens. God calls us to Him through our tears.

✒ *Reflections to Ponder*

Chances are, you are spending time in tears and questioning. Something I've found helpful is writing your questions on a sheet of paper or in a journal. Don't judge them or yourself, just freely write. Unleash them, release them from your heart and mind onto the page. Think of this as a service you are doing yourself—letting the pent-up emotions flow onto the paper through your hand. Let the paper share some of your woes for a while so that you don't have to carry everything inside your heart. Bottled-up grief can make our hearts heavy; sharing it with a friend, even the friend of a journal, can alleviate some of our confusion, frustration, or loneliness.

Next, open your Bible to the book of Psalms and read a few of the ones that pertain to sorrow. Read them aloud. Read the verses that speak to your heart over and over. Mark the verbs that you can relate to. Some that deal with tears and crying out are Psalm 18, 61, and 40.

Prayer

God, meet me. Meet me in my tears. Bring others to walk with me. Sustain me. Lift me up. I want to believe that you are close to the brokenhearted (Ps. 34). Help me in this time of need when it's hard to see straight and even more difficult to have hope. Amen.

When You Walk

As you set out on your walk today, think of the first time you prayed. Where were you? How old were you? Do you recall what your prayer was about?

Two

CALL IT GRIEF

My eyes have grown dim with grief;
my whole frame is but a shadow.
—JOB 17:7

We don't choose grief; it winds itself around us. It damages our eyes with tears, and it entangles our body and our soul. It can make us short of breath, lack energy, and become all-consuming. With horrendous new grief, there is agony, and it feels like there is no escape.

We can grieve the loss of a loved one, and the loss of what we once had. We grieve when we are laid off from a job, when our marriage ends, when our health declines, when a relationship spirals into distrust. We grieve for what we will never have—those dreams that have ended in the snap of a finger.

Our grief becomes the center of our universe. We eat, sleep, and live our sorrow.

Our questions loom: Why me? What did I do to deserve this? How will I survive? How can I continue on with this in my life? Does God love me?

We might feel defeat, regret, remorse, and guilt. There is a cycle of grief-related emotions; often mourners feel they have "recovered" from one only to have it resurface months later.

We are not alone. Others suffer, too. When we realize this and can empathize with others, we've reached a turning point. At chapter meetings of The Compassionate Friends (an organization for bereaved parents and siblings), newcomers are consumed by their struggles. With a certain amount of trepidation and a multitude of vulnerability, they come to a meeting for the first time feeling the weight of their losses. Certain no one has ever felt this badly, they tell how their children or siblings died. It's the seasoned grievers who can reach them and are broad enough in the heart to encompass their pain. People who have already walked similar paths are able to listen and minister to them in ways no one else can.

In our grief, we want to know how others like us have and continue to survive. A mom with a disabled child looks to other parents with disabled children to see how they cope and which strategies they use. When my husband left my three school-aged kids and me one summer day in 2006, I gravitated toward a friend whose husband had recently left her and her daughters. She became a lifeline for me.

Grief may be a solo ride at first, but we are creatures who need to learn from each other. We have a need to hear and see how others have maneuvered through their struggles. This is one of the reasons a support system is vital. God provides for us through the hearts of others.

✍ *Reflections to Ponder*

Is it okay to be upset with God? Does your Christianity allow you to fret with Him? Are you real in your disappointment with God? Perhaps you feel He has let you down. We sing, "What a friend we have in Jesus." How would you talk to a friend who has disappointed you?

Do you need someone (other than Jesus) you can talk with about your current situation who will not judge you or criticize your feelings? Pray for that friend, that God will equip him or her to have time and love for you.

Prayer

Lord, the days are long and I wonder how I'll make it through them. Sometimes I wish I could just crawl away somewhere and not have to deal with any of my problems. Help me to seek You, the Sustainer of my life. I look to You to heal my broken heart. Amen.

When You Walk

Set out to walk today, even if you don't feel like it. Make sure your shoes are comfortable and you are dressed in clothes that allow you to move. As you walk, bring forth your lamentations to God. Cry out to Him. If you walk in a remote area, and no one is around, use your audible voice to present your sorrow to Him.

Three

WHY ME?

How long, LORD? Will you forget me forever?
How long will you hide your face from me?
How long must I wrestle with my thoughts
and day after day have sorrow in my heart?
How long will my enemy triumph over me?

—PSALM 13:1–2

One of the truths about living no one cares to admit is that we have less control over our lives than we realize. While we might always wear a seatbelt when riding in a car, that can only keep us so safe. If a boulder were to fall on top of the car or we were hit by another vehicle, there is no guarantee that our seatbelt would keep us from dying. Perhaps there was a time when we thought that if we trusted God and prayed and went to church and volunteered at VBS, then, surely, we were under God's protection and that He wouldn't let anything bad happen to us.

It was a myth to believe that we would be protected from life's sadness. We live in a broken world and, just as others go through seasons of anguish, so shall we. There are signs of suffering all around us if we open our eyes to them. I used to think bad things only happened to other people. Then one day my son died. Up until his cancer diagnosis he'd been a healthy boy. What caused the tumor? Doctors had no clue. As a mother, I wondered if I'd done something wrong during pregnancy. Was it because I got food poisoning during my sixth month? It must be my fault, something I could have controlled.

Sorrow happens. How will we handle it? Will we ask God to come alongside and walk with us through it? Or will we continue to blame ourselves until we can barely hold our head up?

The sheer vastness and devastation of sorrow is summed up in this quote by Ralph Waldo Emerson: "Sorrow makes us all children again—destroys all differences of intellect. The wisest know nothing."

❧ *Reflections to Ponder*

I've been in grief support groups where fellow bereaved parents have answered the woe, "Why me?" with "Why not me?" Instead of pondering why this bad thing has happened to them, they see that life is filled with many horrible losses, conclude that they are as at risk as anyone else, and, therefore, don't feel they should have been exempted.

While this attitude is commendable, it may not be your current attitude.

Allow yourself to ask the tough questions. Many of these hold no understandable earthly answer. Can you live with not knowing why?

> *Prayer*
>
> God, I pray for a respite from my tears and questions today. Meet me in my struggles.

 ## When You Walk

Take this time to think of others you know who are overwhelmed by life's trials. Set out to pray specifically for those you know who grapple with mental and physical health issues.

Four

THAT FACE
OF ANGER

Pour out your wrath on them;
let your fierce anger overtake them.
—PSALM 69:24

"*I am so consumed with anger; I can feel my blood boil.*"
Chances are there are people who have been instru-
mental in bringing our lives to the unhappy places that
they now are. We point the finger at former bosses for
asking us to pack up our desks and leave the workplace, at
spouses who have broken our trust and denied us love, at
doctors for failing to recognize an ailing parent's need for
new medication, or at a friend who has shot out lies about
us. ANGRY. We see the word when we close our eyes at
night and when we wake each morning. What do we ask

for? Nothing short of payback. *God, pour out your wrath.* We imagine a horned monster breathing out fire at the people who have let us down. *Overtake them!*

What will we do with our anger? We feel it burn inside our veins.

Anger is one of those emotions that is often mistaken as completely negative. From childhood on, we are taught not to show our anger. We are punished for displaying this emotion. Yet, even Jesus got angry. He wept; He lamented; He saw things as they should be but were not and demonstrated his frustration by overturning the tables of the money changers in the temple (Matt. 21:12–13). Of course, even in this action, Jesus didn't sin.

The line between being angry and letting that anger carry over into the territory we call sin is such a fine line. Perhaps if we can couple our anger with verses that remind us of how we are to forgive and love, we can avoid the despair of being consumed with sinful anger. Pray for those who persecute you (Matt. 5:44). Forgive as the Lord forgave you (Col. 3:13). Love never fails (1 Cor. 13:8).

❧ *Reflections to Ponder*

Seclude yourself in a room where no one can hear you. Set a timer for three minutes and let yourself think about your anger. Scream, rant, and rave. When the timer dings, stand up, take a breath, and then partake in another action. Each day, anger may build up. Allow yourself time to deal with it and release it.

On a piece of paper or in your journal, write out your anger. You may write the names of people you might be frustrated with or particular situations. Sometimes it is helpful to write a letter to the person you are upset with. Many find that after writing the letter, tearing it up symbolizes the ability to let it go.

Of all the things you've heard about anger, do you feel it can be justified? When does it cross a line and become too much, too consuming?

Prayer

Lord, please don't let my anger keep me from hearing from You or from desiring what You want for me in my life. I know You love me. I may not feel it right now, but I know from Scripture verses that Your love for me is beyond my comprehension. Thank you, Lord, for Your love. Amen.

When You Walk

When something has happened and I get angry, I like to walk. Walking not only provides me with some needed exercise, it helps me let off steam and I can do it without harming anyone. As the endorphins are going and I share my frustration with God, my mind becomes clearer.

As you set out on your walk today, spend some time with your anger. Then think of what the word *blessings* means to you. What do you think of as blessings? How often do you think of blessings? How does your current loss keep you from focusing on anything pleasing? What can you do to change that? If you cannot feel positively about anything right now, can you hope that one day you will?

Five

ANGER REVISITED

Refrain from anger and turn from wrath;
do not fret—it leads only to evil.
—PSALM 37:8

here are times when anger holds a different face from the one that wants to lash out and destroy.

I am angry when I read my local paper and see that someone else has been the victim of theft or abuse. We can hold anger for a system that has failed us, for a political party that has not been honest.

We can be angry for the things that are not of God. Recently, a young girl was the victim of a drive-by shooting. She was innocently standing in a driveway when a car came by and a gun was fired at her. The bullet was meant for someone else, but she was killed. I am angry that this happened. My heart mourns her loss.

Others in my town did something productive with their anger. Since the victim's family couldn't afford a headstone, people in the community raised money for it. Channeling our anger so that it can be used for good is certainly an excellent way to deal with the injustices we see on a day-to-day basis. I'm angry when I look at childhood cancer statistics and see that kids are still dying from malignant tumors in this country.

When my son first died, I contributed to a childhood cancer foundation in his name. By promoting a research event or a fund drive for a cause we find worthy, we are allowing our anger to be used for a positive purpose.

Reflections to Ponder

The psalms are filled with anger and with wanting God to do something against enemies. Jesus asks us to love those who wrong us. Who can you forgive today?

Prayer

Read Psalm 37. Let the verses you read be your prayer today.

Do not fret because of evil men
or be envious of those who do wrong;
for like the grass they will soon wither,
like green plants they will soon die away.

Trust in the LORD and do good;
dwell in the land and enjoy safe pasture.

> *Delight yourself in the LORD*
> *and he will give you the desires of your heart.*
> (vv. 1–4)

 ## When You Walk

View the plants, trees, and flowers as you walk today. Though beautiful, these flowers will wither and die. The trees filled with leaves will lose those leaves, and after they fall, the leaves will be raked and tossed out with the yard waste.

Life on this earth is short. What kind of legacy do you wish to leave?

Six

HAVE I BEEN FORSAKEN?

Record my misery;
list my tears in your scroll—
are they not in your record?
—PSALM 56:8

hen C. S. Lewis' wife died, he wrote: "No one ever told me that grief felt so like fear."

As we plough through our days—either with energy or without—we are surprised at how scary the world can seem. Where is God in all of this? I used to feel close to Him, but lately, He seems like He's left the building.

Questions bombard our minds. Why is He silent? Why don't I feel Him? What is wrong with Him? What is wrong with me? Our self-esteem might falter, especially when we hear testimonies of how He's blessed others around us with jobs, with health, and with loving relationships.

In his book, *A Grief Observed*, C. S. Lewis also writes, "When you are happy, so happy you have no sense of needing Him, so happy that you are tempted to feel His claims upon you as an interruption, if you remember yourself and turn to Him with gratitude and praise, you will be—or so it feels—welcomed with open arms. But go to Him when your need is desperate, when all other help is vain, and what do you find? A door slammed in your face, and a sound of bolting and double bolting on the inside. After that, silence" (18).

We might conclude that we aren't the ones with the problem. We might neglect to remember that we do live in a sin-filled world where, often, things are not as we believe they should be. We believe we are entitled to the happiness others feel, and, since our present turmoil keeps us from happiness, something is therefore wrong with God.

Even Jesus asked His Father why He had been forsaken. I think we can assume that Jesus felt abandoned.

Yet we know the outcome of the Crucifixion story. God was working in the midst of the agony and pain Jesus suffered. Can we trust that God works even when He seems silent? Can we believe that He sees each tear, perhaps even numbers them as He has the hairs on our heads?

✍ *Reflections to Ponder*

The fear of being left out in the cold grips us. Spend some time focusing on the promises we are given.

So do not fear, for I am with you;
> *do not be dismayed, for I am your God.*
I will strengthen you and help you;
> *I will uphold you with my righteous right hand.*
(Isa. 41:10)

Come near to God and he will come near to you.
(James 4:8)

Can you write these promises on your heart?

Prayer

Lord, help me to see that even in the silence and pain of my situation, Your love for me is vast. You uphold me with everlasting arms. Others might forsake me, but You will never leave.

❧ *When You Walk*

Pretend Jesus is your walking partner today. Envision Him as a person dressed in exercise gear. His strides match yours. What does He say to you? What do you say to Him?

Seven

RESCUE ME!

. . . my eyes are dim with grief.
I call to you, O LORD, every day;
I spread out my hands to you.

—PSALM 88:9

Observing a temper tantrum in a child is no easy feat.
We watch a child asking for a cookie, and then when
denied she continues to beg, and then the begging leads
to wailing. Nine times out of ten, kicking and scream-
ing follow. Sometimes the only way to stop the escalating
behavior is to pick the child up and hold her until she, at
last, is exhausted and settles in her parent's arms.

As adults, often we're still like a child. We vacillate
between wanting to pull away, storm out, go our own way,
and wanting to be rescued from ourselves. Somebody hold

me, help me take my eyes off of me and my dilemma and focus on something else.

At times, like a child, we get to a place where we are totally out of sorts, unable to even see or think clearly anymore. Life seems to have swallowed us whole. We are in dire need of help.

Open your eyes and look to the One who is standing beside you, His arms outstretched. He wants to pick you up and hold you until your tears and frustration cease.

When a mother came back home from a Mary Kay party with more makeup on than she usually wore, her four-year-old daughter stood at a distance for a moment before running into her arms. Then smiling into her face, the child said, "I know it's you, Mommy! I know you're in there."

While you might put on a new façade in the form of a different hairstyle or article of clothing, you can't fool those who are closest to you. They still recognize you. How much more acquainted with you is God! He knows you better than you know yourself. He loves you more than anyone ever can or will.

Reflections to Ponder

Close your eyes and spread out your hands. Lift them up over your head. Stretch them out in front of you, palms up. Imagine God reaching out for you. Spend a few moments in silence. Listen for God's stirrings in your heart. Close and then open your hands as though you are giving your concerns over to God.

Read aloud Psalm 88:9: "... my eyes are dim with grief. I call to you, O Lord, every day; I spread out my hands to you."

In response to this verse, read also Psalm 18:19: "He [the Lord] brought me into a spacious place; he rescued me because he delighted in me."

If you are overwhelmed by what you feel your life is lacking or what you think is not right, jot down your concerns. Sometimes releasing your pent-up discontent helps because you are getting it out of your mind and letting the paper hold the weight of it. What troubles you? Can you put your fears on paper? Do you believe that the Lord will counsel you as you seek Him (Ps. 16:7)?

Prayer

Save me for I am drowning.
Save me for I worry.
Save me for I fear.
Save me for I am consumed with despair.
Save me, O God.
You have rescued me
from drowning,
from worry,
from fear,
and from despair.
Thank you, O God.

✎ *When You Walk*

Find a park to walk to and a place to sit. On a note pad, list what you know about God to be true. How will you implement these truths in your daily life?

SECTION TWO

Sustained to Nurture

Eight

GENTLENESS MIXED WITH MERCY

Be merciful to me, O LORD, for I am in distress;
my eyes grow weak with sorrow,
my soul and body with grief.

—PSALM 31:9

eing kind and gentle in our grief is important so that we can be a friend to ourselves. We may feel so exhausted from the *couldas*, *shouldas*, and *wouldas* that we reprimand and berate ourselves for the mistakes we've made and the guilt we feel. Even in our agony, we must be kind enough to push ourselves out of bed and get moving so that we can focus on our healing. A friend who fractured her leg told me that she firmly believes a healthy attitude helps us heal. As she goes to rehab sessions, she focuses on the positive.

On your bad days, tell yourself that no matter what unhappy circumstance you are in, you will not give in to playing the role of *the victim*. With God on your side, you are not a hopeless wreck. Even if you hear the old adage "God helps those who help themselves" and feel that trusting in God is not "doing enough" to remedy your situation, refrain from self-loathing and harsh judgment. And by the way, although people toss the "God helps those" reference around like a familiar Bible verse, there is no verse in the Bible that matches it.

One of the beautiful attributes about God is that He does not deal with us as we deserve (Ps. 103:10). He is, instead, merciful: ". . . a God of forgiveness, gracious and merciful, slow to become angry, and rich in unfailing love" (Neh. 9:17 NLT). "The Lord is full of compassion and mercy" (James 5:11). "Be merciful, just as your Father is merciful" (Luke 6:36). Likewise, agree to be gentle and show mercy to yourself.

Sometimes I am my own worst enemy. My expectations are high and I feel I don't meet them. At times like these, I'm reminded of an afternoon when I ran into a young pastor friend. As he stood from the table of the outdoor café to hug me and introduce me to his friend, he said, "This is Alice. She's an author. And an all-around wonderful person."

That day, we had been in the middle of another one of our many household mega upheavals (whoever said that a stepdad and teen stepkids learn to adapt to each other in a few weeks?). In spite of feeling the weight of inadequacy and dismay, in that moment I felt worth something. Perhaps God Himself had supplied those words for my friend. Perhaps God Himself believed them.

Reflections to Ponder

Can you believe that God is for you? He cheers you on to continue to follow Him, find Him, learn, make mistakes, be forgiven, get up, and continue. How will you experience His love today?

Prayer

May I let this be my prayer:

For I am convinced that neither death nor life, neither angels nor demons, neither the present nor the future, nor any powers, neither height nor depth, nor anything else in all creation, will be able to separate us from the love of God that is in Christ Jesus our LORD (Rom. 8:38–39).

Amen.

✑ *When You Walk*

For every "what if" you have spinning through your mind, quote Psalm 103:8–10 NLT:

> *The LORD is compassionate and merciful,*
>   *slow to get angry and filled with*
> *unfailing love.*
> *He will not constantly accuse us,*
>   *nor remain angry forever.*
> *He does not punish us for all our sins;*
>   *he does not deal harshly with us, as*
> *we deserve.*

With each step you take, let these verses be your mantra today.

Nine

LOVING ME!

I praise you because I am fearfully
and wonderfully made;
your works are wonderful,
I know that full well.

—PSALM 139:14

Genuine self-love is needed in order to be able to love others and to love God. Take care of the vessel God created. We are a temple!

Some days we forget that God created us in His image. We neglect to remember that we are His workmanship created in Christ Jesus. *Your works are wonderful*, David confesses in this psalm. If God's works are wonderful and we are one of His works, then we, too, are wonderful.

Uncomfortable and unhappy events have intruded on your life. Perhaps you have experienced the death of a loved one, or divorce. Perhaps a child has cut ties with you or is in dire straits. You might feel at fault. You feel attacked by your shortcomings. Self-loathing can kick in, like a poison, and pretty soon you have denied yourself of any worth.

Look up! You are not a plastic bag blown by the wind. You are valued!

As you need to be loved, you also can give love (1 John 4:7–8).

Reflections to Ponder

Can you see the beauty you are as a child of the King?

How do we love ourselves in light of God's perfection?

How will you take care of yourself today? Through exercise? Through nutrition? Through prayer? Through keeping negativisms at bay?

Prayer

Yes, I do need forgiveness and I ask for You, dear God, to silence me for a moment so that I can bring my sins to You. I list some of them now. Yet, even in my sin, Your love for me is unfathomable. I thank You that You forgive and love so freely.

When You Walk

Every few paces, list an attribute about yourself. Are you kind? Compassionate? Have a heart for the poor or those in prison?

List one about God.

Keep repeating this pattern as you walk.

You might not feel worthy or loved or lovable. But the same God with the attributes you listed loves you and gave you the attributes you find within yourself. He has knit you with Him. As you walk, think of how you know that He has not given up on you, nor is He finished with you. You are a work of art in progress.

Ten

ADAPTING

But I trust in your unfailing love;
my heart rejoices in your salvation.
—PSALM 13:5

I equate adapting in a raw season of life to a game of tennis. Only in this game the opponents are many and have the capacity to lob balls at you at a constant clip. The balls have names on them like *Insensitive Comment* or *Preachy Attitude*, as well as a host of questions that cause your skin to crawl. If you're going through a divorce, the balls are named *Failure* and *Defeat*, and some speak to you in lengthy phrases like, "I've been married twenty-nine years to the same man. We believe in staying together till death do us part. We don't give up like so many couples do these days."

In the course of a day, circumstances, words, clichés, and memories are presented to you in the form of these balls. Your job is to hit each ball with your racket. By lobbing at the balls you are trying to keep any from hitting you. You don't want to spend any time letting the words on the balls keep you from doing your tasks for the day. Knocking them away from your court and back over the net is your goal.

This is how I lived after my son died. By the end of the day, I was exhausted and ready to pour out my frustrations into my journal. My first journals are filled with the many unnecessary words that well-meaning folks (and some not so well-meaning) tossed my way. "Be glad he's in a better place." "God needed another flower in His garden." "At least you have other children." "God doesn't give us more than we can handle." "The best place for our children is at the feet of Jesus, and that's where your Daniel is now." Seeing a family of six out at a restaurant or hearing a commercial for St. Jude's Children's Hospital also made me swing my racket.

When we are in a new situation, the landscape is uncharted. The only way to survive is to learn to cope with our situation. Cultivating coping mechanisms is vital to getting through the early days. While we are tempted to stay in bed all day so that we don't have to face new comments and criticisms, we know we can't live that way permanently. We have to rise. The ways to get up and get moving may be simplistic, like treating ourselves to a cup of good coffee or a hot shower with our favorite body wash.

Coping with the day's challenges may also come in the forms of support groups or the weekly help of a therapist. Words are powerful, words can encourage or discourage. Let the words you speak to yourself be uplifting and as energizing as Psalm 146:

Praise the LORD.

Praise the LORD, O my soul.
I will praise the LORD all my life;
    I will sing praise to my God as long as I live.

Do not put your trust in princes,
    in mortal men, who cannot save.
When their spirit departs, they return to the ground;
    on that very day their plans come to nothing.

Blessed is he whose help is the God of Jacob,
    whose hope is in the LORD his God,
the Maker of heaven and earth,
    the sea, and everything in them—
    the LORD, who remains faithful forever.
He upholds the cause of the oppressed
    and gives food to the hungry.
The LORD sets the prisoners free,
    the LORD gives sight to the blind,
the LORD lifts up those who are bowed down,
    the LORD loves the righteous.
The LORD watches over the alien
    and sustains the fatherless and the widow,
    but he frustrates the ways of the wicked.

The LORD reigns forever,
    your God, O Zion, for all generations.

Praise the LORD.

Combat the negative thoughts by telling yourself affirmations each hour. Hopefully you will start to believe them.

Sometimes, in our frustration with our situations, we need to find ways to channel our negative energy. Walking at least three miles a day helps me. Jog, play tennis, play the saxophone, mow the grass. Get out there and get moving. Befriend the poor, the hungry, the widow, the fatherless, the prisoners, the alien. Find someone else who is suffering and affirm them in the love of our Lord.

Reflections to Ponder

Keep a journal. Studies show writing reduces stress and if you write at least five times a week for twenty minutes you will notice the affects.

Also, try to envision your current situation as you would like to see it. Picture your kids getting along with your new spouse. Imagine peaceful conversations and the acceptance of each other. Pray for this to take place and keep praying that one day it will.

Prayer

"What matters is not what we feel like praying about, but what God wants us to ask him for. Not

> the poverty of our own heart, but the riches of the Word of God must decide how we are to pray." (Bonhoeffer, *Life Together*, 157)

When You Walk

As you walk, think of those in the Bible who went through transitions in their journey and learned to adapt. Moses is a great example of someone who was brought up by God for a specific mission—to deliver His people out of captivity in Egypt. Yet, even though God spoke to him in a burning bush, Moses pleaded with his Lord to send someone else to accomplish this task. Moses didn't accept or adjust to God's plan for him overnight. It took time for him to grow into the role and be transformed.

Do you believe that God can transform you in your situation?

Eleven

LETTING GO

Be still, and know that I am God...
—PSALM 46:10

We often want to carry our pain or wear it like a badge of honor. See me in my misery. Hear my cries. I have it so bad.

And yes, we do have it bad. We have been hurt, wounded, treated unfairly, and may feel abandoned by God, family, or friends. Oh, if we could only crawl into a hole and disappear. Get me out of this mess!

Yet, each day we wake to face another day—still here to deal with our pain.

In our deep misery we may either call out to God or ignore Him. Either way, we need help. One day, looking in the mirror, we realize that we have to do something. We can't keep keeping on like this.

Submit to God. Flee the devil. Put aside your plans for a moment and concentrate on who God is. Start each day fresh with, "In the morning, O Lord, you hear my voice; in the morning I lay my requests before you and wait in expectation" (Ps. 5:3).

Expect of God. There is no room for doubt. What He does might not be exactly what you have in mind. His ways may not coincide with your plan. But He is with you in your situation and His love for you is beyond measure.

Will you believe?

Reflections to Ponder

Imagine that you are seated on the shore beside a lake. The season is late spring, and the trees are abundant with growth. Jesus suddenly comes to you walking on the water. He invites you to stand up and walk out to meet Him. What do you do? What do you fear? What do you say to Jesus? How does He respond?

Prayer

Lord, this is my prayer today:

How long, O Lord? Will you forget me forever?
How long will you hide your face from me?
How long must I wrestle with my thoughts
and day after day have sorrow in my heart?
How long will my enemy triumph over me?

> *Look on me and answer, O LORD my God.*
>   *Give light to my eyes, or I will sleep in death;*
> *my enemy will say, "I have overcome him,"*
>   *and my foes will rejoice when I fall.*
>
> *But I trust in your unfailing love;*
>   *my heart rejoices in your salvation.*
> *I will sing to the LORD,*
>   *for he has been good to me. (Ps. 13)*

 ### When You Walk

Think about ways you can rejoice in your salvation.

Twelve

FORGIVING MYSELF AND OTHERS

Jesus said, "Father, forgive them,
for they do not know what they are doing."
And they divided up his clothes by casting lots.
—LUKE 23:34

We mess up. We say the wrong thing. We harbor resentment and it comes out in a series of blaming others. We can't forgive the doctor or the neighbor. They should have known better. We can't forgive ourselves for failing. We're judgmental, haughty, self-serving.

I know that I neglect to spend enough time throughout the year thinking about Jesus and His death on the cross. Good Friday and Easter come and I reflect, but I don't live a Good Friday and Easter lifestyle. Society tends to do the same. We all let what Jesus has done fill only a segment of our daily routines. How much better off we'd be if we embraced the Crucifixion each day and remembered that, even at His weakest moment, Jesus knew the value of forgiving those who persecuted and ridiculed Him. I'm moved by what a gracious example of love He showed. And right behind that thought always follows—I wonder how He was able to demonstrate such a lavish act.

True, we have a long way to go to show the Jesus kind of forgiveness. But we can certainly strive to encompass forgiveness and learn how to better go about putting it into our daily lives.

Jesus said if you want to be forgiven, you need to forgive. As we realize our own mistakes and need for God's grace, we are humbled. Can we also forgive as we are forgiven? Perhaps first we need to practice forgiving ourselves for our mistakes, however small or large. After this act of repentance, we can turn to God and express the difficulty we have in forgiving others. Ask Him to help with this monumental struggle to forgive you might be experiencing. "Forgive as the LORD forgave you" (Col. 3:13).

What does forgiveness do for us? Forgiving ourselves and others frees us to experience the blessings God has in store for us. If resentment takes permanent root in our hearts, it steals. Each day it clutches at the fibers of our heart; it spreads, taking us away from life-giving and life-flowing resources that our bodies and minds need, like love, joy, humility, and grace. I cringe at how often I've allowed my stubbornness of holding onto my resentment to cause me to miss the blessings.

Reflections to Ponder

Reading about others and the hope they found through forgiveness is beneficial. I recommend two books set in World War II, both written by Holocaust survivors: Corrie Ten Boom's *The Hiding Place* and Viktor Frankl's *Man's Search for Meaning.*

When a teen broke into our home and stole our cars three times in the same month, I was relieved when he was brought to justice. However, his mother would not pay the deductible on the insurance policy for the Ford Focus that was never recovered by the police. My insurance claims man was sure she'd pay, and when he called to tell me she wasn't going to, I fought anger. In court she said she was going on a cruise. Surely she has money to pay the deductible. But, at last, I held the letter saying she would not pay up over my head, tore it into shreds, and let the pieces scatter onto my kitchen floor. This action symbolized for me that I would no longer let my anger toward her steal anymore from me.

Prayer

Pray this benediction for yourself and for those who have wronged you: "May the grace of the

Lord Jesus Christ, and the love of God, and the fellowship of the Holy Spirit be with you all" (2 Cor. 13:14). Grace. Love. Fellowship.

 ## *When You Walk*

Spend time thinking about the power of the Holy Spirit in your life. As you set out on your walk today, ask that the Holy Spirit bring to your mind a person you need to forgive. Perhaps this is someone you hold a grudge against because of what he or she has done to you in the past. This person may or may not be aware of the pain he or she has brought to you. Either way, ask for your heart to be softened toward this person. If you can, pray for God's blessings for that person.

Thirteen

Renewing My Mind

Finally, brothers and sisters, whatever is true,
whatever is noble, whatever is right,
whatever is pure, whatever is lovely,
whatever is admirable—
if anything is excellent or praiseworthy—
think about such things.
—PHILIPPIANS 4:8

Waking each day to disturbing thoughts that internally defeat your spirit can be exhausting. Whether due to financial crises or agony over the death of a loved one, getting motivated to face another day is wearying.

"I encourage others," my friend Gina said at lunch the other day. "But when it comes to me, I realize that my words towards myself are negative."

I understand my friend so well that at my desk I have a note card that reads, *"Only Positive!"* I believe in calling things as they are and admitting that circumstances aren't always rosy, but self-negativity does not work. Ever. If you want to break through the fog of self-discouragement, start today. Make a conscious effort to speak affirmations that give life to your spirit.

We have to protect our minds from taking on those thought patterns that lead to ruin. Our minds are sharp, smart, but also extremely vulnerable. And when we are in a stressful situation or lacking sleep or good nutrition, they are even more subject to weakness. The next thing we know we are feeling worse about ourselves because, instead of observing the cues that have led us toward negativity, we have let our minds venture down those destructive roads. Fight it! Stop those thoughts before they take root. This is the time to hang out a sign that says to our brains: *Access Denied.* Chose life-giving thoughts instead.

We remember that our God is not one who changes with our thoughts or our feelings. As fickle humans, we slide between feelings of happiness, joy, trust, sadness, and dismay. One day, usually a sunny spring day when the purple lilacs are in bloom, I might feel optimistic, carefree, and my trust in God soars. The next day, I might wake with a headache, back pain, and a heavy heart because of a friend's recent diagnosis. In all honesty, I find myself admitting, "I don't feel God." But the good news is God is not a mere *feeling*. He isn't any stronger because we feel Him or any weaker when we don't.

So, in spite of our sorrow, we hope. I often think that we are creatures of hope, somehow believing as Orphan Annie did when she sang, "Tomorrow! The sun will come out, tomorrow!" We hope that each new day will be better than yesterday, that it might be the day for things to change for the better. And when we run out of that *feeling* of hope, we rest in the *knowledge* that God is forever God—His promises do not change, His faithfulness reaches beyond the stars. His truth sets us free.

Reflections to Ponder

What are some truths?

What is pure?

What do you find admirable?

What can you praise God for?

Prayer

Take a look at other verses in the fourth chapter of Philippians. The last verses show us what to think about, and the passage ends with a promise: "The God of peace will be with you." Let this be your prayer today.

Rejoice in the Lord always. I will say it again: Rejoice! Let your gentleness be evident to all. The

---

Lord is near. Do not be anxious about anything, but in every situation, by prayer and petition, with thanksgiving, present your requests to God. And the peace of God, which transcends all understanding, will guard your hearts and your minds in Christ Jesus.

Finally, brothers and sisters, whatever is true, whatever is noble, whatever is right, whatever is pure, whatever is lovely, whatever is admirable— if anything is excellent or praiseworthy—think about such things. Whatever you have learned or received or heard from me, or seen in me—put it into practice. And the God of peace will be with you. (Phil. 4:4–9)

When You Walk

Sure, we can look at others and note their wonderful attributes, but it is also important to thank God for how He has made you! There is no one like you and you are the best at being you. As you walk, think of your strengths. What do others find attractive about you? Ask God what He finds delightful about you. Listen.

How can you use your strengths to reach others today?

Fourteen

RESTING

Find rest, O my soul, in God alone;
my hope comes from him.
—PSALM 62:5

*I*n our American society, resting might be equated with laziness. So how do we justify resting in a busy world?

If ever we have lost the ability to rest, it is now. We have believed the myth that by spinning our wheels we can accomplish more and become more productive. We use lines like, "I'm so busy." Others describe someone by saying, "Oh, she's so busy. She has so much going on." This is considered a virtue. I have come to hate hearing the "I'm so busy" phrase and refuse to use it about myself. A friend once told me, "We are never too busy to do what we want to do," and I believe this. We all have twenty-four hours in a day; for the most part we fill them with what we want to do. So it's not like Mr. or Ms. Busy has taken us over like we are some victim; we have chosen and selected what we want to make us occupied.

For seventeen months, I taught English at a refugee camp in the Philippines. To a newcomer, the Southeast Asian refugees appeared to have it easy. While it was mandatory that they attend English classes each day, the rest of their days were spent in doing what they wanted. They weren't employed. Aside from going to the market to get food and cook meals for their families, their lives appeared tranquil.

Yet sometimes it is what we can't see that is more real than what we can. The refugees were a displaced people, having to leave their war-torn homelands of Cambodia, Laos, and Vietnam. They spent time in the camp reflecting on their plight and sharing stories of where they had been and where they were headed. The months in the camp were a time of gaining strength. The rest was needed in order to prepare for new customs, new ventures, and new challenges in the United States. The Christian refugees spent time in prayer for one another.

It is not our busyness that makes us more lovable or more cherished by God. He already loves us all that He can with His good and perfect love. Our works don't gain extra love from Him. In fact, He called His disciples over to get some rest. In Mark 6:31, Jesus said, "'Come with me by yourselves to a quiet place and get some rest.'" Rest has been and always will be needed. Our resting time doesn't have to be idle time. We can choose to use it to draw near to God and to look to Him to fill us with His healing love.

A respite for me is going out on our boat, *Rain Song*, named after my first novel. As my husband Carl steers the twenty-two-foot runabout over Falls Lake, I sit in the bow, the wind brushing across my face. We zip past boats and view the trees on the shore, swimming geese, and an occasional hawk. Riding on our boat is a time when I reflect, pray, and get ideas for my books. When I'm on this cozy fiberglass vessel, I feel transported to another place, free from the restraints of time, united with nature, and at peace.

Reflections to Ponder

Take time to rest. Ponder. Reflect. Dream. Pray. Do you have a place of sanctuary where you can go? If not, create a place so that you can retreat to it for times of rest. It could be a park bench or even a favorite chair in your den. Let this be a place where you are free to mourn, to cry, to remember, to sing.

Prayer

In times of storms, grant me rest.
In times of sickness, grant me rest.
In times of heartache, grant me rest.
In times of fear, grant me rest.
In times of anger, grant me rest.

In times of uncertainty, grant me rest.
In times of regret, grant me rest.

 ## When You Walk

What can you do to nourish your soul today? How can you be more firmly rooted in God?

Fifteen

OUR DAILY BREAD

God is not human, that he should lie,
not a human being, that he should change his mind.
Does he speak and then not act?
Does he promise and not fulfill?

—NUMBERS 23:19

*S*ights from growing up linger in our minds even as adults. My missionary neighbor had the well-known framed picture of the old white-bearded man bowing his head beside a table laden with a loaf of bread, a thick book, a knife, and a pair of old spectacles. Recently I visited a friend, and she had the same picture on her wall. To me, this picture (the first image you find when you Google "Our Daily Bread" on images) is what I like to envision when I ask God to supply my daily needs. The man is worn, old, but wise. I know he's wise because he knows the source of his strength.

I, too, have learned the source of my sustenance. It is the posture of closing my eyes, folding my hands, bowing my head, and talking to God. It's the act of trusting my Father to meet my needs. Each day.

I like to think of the Israelites as they traveled towards the Promised Land. God provided them with manna. Daily, they were given this bread from Heaven, and told to gather as much as was needed (Exod. 16:21). They could bake the manna or boil it.

But there was one stipulation—one coming as a command God imparted to His servant Moses. No one was to keep any of this bread from Heaven till morning. In other words, no hoarding allowed! Yet, some of the people were tempted to think that God might forget or that He wouldn't come through the next day. So they hoarded the manna. God let them know that hoarding was not going to work. The extra manna they tried to hide for the next day ended up being infested with maggots and produced a foul odor. *Uh-oh. Should have listened. Now I have to spend my Tuesday cleaning out my tent.* Only the night before the Sabbath (Friday) were folks instructed to gather enough for both that day and the Sabbath. And sure enough, to keep the Sabbath holy, no manna floated down from the sky on the day of rest (Exod. 16:23–30). And, surprisingly, the extra amount collected did not rot.

Coupled with this account, I like to think of the verse from Psalm 119. Verse 105: "Your word is a lamp to my feet and a light for my path." Old lamps or torches from this time period only shed enough light for the next step. These torches didn't provide enough light for the long distance path. When we journey with God, we seldom get to see the whole picture, the entire course we are to take. We only get light on a small portion, and that portion is enough for the day.

The New Testament also emphasizes the need to rid ourselves of worry, and instead put on the cloak of trust. In Matthew chapter 6, Jesus tells those who were there to hear Him not to worry about what they would eat or drink or even wear. The birds of the air get what they need for each day, and we are more valuable than they are.

Each morning, God is asking, "Do you trust Me? Do you really trust Me?" And we think we do. We certainly know that trusting Him makes sense. We know there is no one else we can depend on, rely on, and lean on. But, oh, why is it so complicated when the rubber meets the road?

I find it easier to trust God for the fruits of the spirit—peace, patience, and kindness—than it is to trust Him with my finances. When my bank account gets low, I have been known to panic, picturing my family huddled around me out on the streets with knapsacks on our backs. If I truly believe God is the provider of all our daily needs, why does the need for finances prevent me from trusting as easily? As if I needed patience instead? I tell others I have no reason to doubt; God has given to me in numerous and creative ways, albeit it is usually at the eleventh hour. *Oh Lord, grow me in this area.*

Listen as He encourages you: Let Me guide you, be with you, mature you; let Me be your Father. All you need is called "enough for today."

Reflections to Ponder

Fill a basket with a loaf of bread. Fill a glass with water. Set them side by side. Pull up a chair and close your eyes. Ask God to help you trust Him to fill your life with just what you need for each day.

Prayer

Our Father who art in Heaven,
Hallowed be thy name.
Thy kingdom come,
Thy will be done,
On earth as it is in Heaven.
Give us this day
Our daily bread,
And forgive our debts
As we forgive our debtors.
Lead us not into temptation,
But deliver us from evil.
For thine is the kingdom,
And the power, and the glory forever.
Amen.

When You Walk

Look up! Manna comes from Heaven, not by your scouring the ground for leftover crumbs. Keep your head up. Be encouraged!

Fill your mind with the characteristics of God. In the psalms He is known as my rock (Ps. 28), my light and my salvation (Ps. 27), my shepherd (Ps. 23), and my strength, my fortress, and my deliverer, as well as my shield and the horn of my salvation (Ps. 18).

Make a list of these and other references to the character of God. Read and recall them each day.

Sixteen

I Choose
to Trust

Therefore I tell you, do not worry about your life,
what you will eat or drink;
or about your body, what you will wear.
Is not life more than food,
and the body more important than clothes?

—Matthew 6:25

One of my friends wrote the word trust across her knuckles as a reminder. Each time she looked at the back of her hand, she remembered she had chosen to trust God and not to despair.

When others hear of our current dismal situations, they might casually say, "Oh, just trust God." While they might be sincere, they might not have been in a predicament like yours. All of their children might still be healthy and living. They may have plenty of money to pay their bills, and these "just-trusters" may have husbands or wives whispering in their ears how wonderful they are and teens who not only keep their rooms clean, but dust, vacuum, and mop the whole house.

Don't let them make you think that there is anything wrong with you for having a hard time trusting God in the bleakness of your days. Read the psalms and you'll see that even the psalmists struggled with fully diving into God's arms to rest.

However, even in your suffering, an attitude of deep trust can germinate. God can bring you to an abundant trust in Him, a trust in which your attitude thrives with the knowledge that, although situations seem humanly unbearable, you know He sustains.

One of the ways He does this is by providing you with the gift of commitment. As the familiar song goes, "I have decided to follow Jesus. No turning back, no turning back." He is the one I have committed my life to. Therefore, even in adversity, I will keep my relationship with Jesus strong.

To illustrate this, I'm going to share with you the story of the carrot, the egg, and the coffee bean—a tale that has circled its way around the Internet. You've probably seen it. This is how it goes in my paraphrased attempt:

> A young woman visited her mom one afternoon with tears, complaining that life was just too hard and that she wanted to give up. "I get one problem

resolved and another one comes up," she said as her mother handed her a tissue.

Then her mother took her to the kitchen. She filled three pots with water and placed each on a burner and set the flames under them. In the first pot she placed carrots, in the second she placed eggs, and in the last she placed ground coffee beans. She let them boil as her daughter wondered what was going on.

About twenty minutes later, the mother turned off the burners. She fished the carrots out and put them in a bowl. She took out the eggs and set them in a bowl. Then she ladled the coffee out and placed it in a bowl. Turning to her daughter, she asked, "Tell me what you see."

The girl wondered if her mother was going crazy. Was this a trick question? "Carrots, eggs, and coffee," she said. Then, following her mother's cue, she felt the soft carrot. She took an egg and broke it. After peeling off the shell, she observed the hard-boiled egg. She tasted the water with the coffee beans in them. "Okay, Mom," the daughter said, "What are you trying to tell me?"

Her mother explained that each of these objects had faced the same adversity: boiling water. Each reacted differently to the challenge.

The carrot went in strong, hard, and unrelenting. However, after being subjected to the boiling water, it softened and became weak.

The egg had been fragile. Its thin outer shell had protected its liquid interior, but after sitting through the boiling water, its insides became hardened.

The ground coffee beans were unique. After they'd spent time in the boiling water, they had changed the water.

"Which are you?" she asked her daughter. "When adversity knocks on your door, how do you respond? Are you a carrot, an egg, or a coffee bean? When the water gets hot, the coffee bean releases the fragrance and flavor. If you are like the bean, when things are at their worst, you get better and change the situation around you. When the hour is the darkest and trials are their greatest, do you elevate yourself to another level? How do you handle adversity? Are you a carrot, an egg, or a coffee bean?"

I imagine that the daughter got the point of the story and vowed from then on to be a coffee bean.

✏ *Reflections to Ponder*

Think of an action you can take to entrust God with your fears. If you step up to the plate believing God will meet you, what do you expect to encounter? What are the assurances you hold? Your fears?

Write a word or two describing an attribute of God on a note card. If you're artistic, write the words in fancy letters and color them with markers. Keep the note card by your bedside or computer and read it aloud each day.

Prayer

I make my decision to trust You again today, Lord. The path may look rocky and uncertain, but I have chosen to trust You. Help me know that You hold my hand as I go about my tasks this day.

When You Walk

What do you find hard to give over to God? Are you fearful of what He might ask of you if you surrender? Is trusting God hard for you to do because of that voice inside your head that whispers, "What if this time He doesn't come through?" Ask God to remind you of specific times in the past when He was faithful when you looked to Him for help.

Seventeen

LAUGHTER

Our mouths were filled with laughter,
our tongues with songs of joy.
—PSALM 126:2

y husband and I were just getting over one of our arguments when we stopped at a Burger King on the West Virginia Turnpike. Carl entered the restaurant to buy us lunch and returned to the car to hand me a drink in a cup and a small paper bag. The first thing I saw when I peered into the bag was a pink toy wrapped in plastic. Laughing, I pulled the figurine out—a little girl with ponytails and a wand. Unwrapping her, I secured a pair of combs in the shape of wings onto her back. Still laughing, I turned her head and moved her arms.

Did my laughter help our moods? Yes. Later, when we were discussing attributes we appreciated about each other, Carl said he liked that I could be excited and laugh over a toy in a kid's meal. (During a visit to my local elementary school the next week this same little girl greeted me from the cover of an illustrated book, *Pinkalicious*. Since then I've read all about Pinkalicious and her desire to stay true to herself.)

It's only been in my adult life that I have been able to picture our God as a God of laughter. How thankful I am that He created laughter. And unlike chocolate cake, laughter provides a healthy workout for your facial muscles, diaphragm, and abdomen. It can also be contagious. What can be the harm in that? Unless, of course, it starts to ripple too loudly during a somber church service.

Oh, that we may embrace this gift, especially in the midst of our heartbreak. Like a good medicine, it alleviates our pain, even if only temporarily, and lightens our heavy circumstances.

✎ *Reflections to Ponder*

Abandon your worries for a moment and let yourself laugh. Watch a movie or spend time with a toddler. Read to a three-year-old. Look for the amusing and the fun in life. Take time to relax and enjoy. Learn to laugh at yourself. When you can laugh at your forgetfulness or folly, you can also forgive yourself easier, realizing that, just like everyone else, you are human. Post a note card by your desk with the words "a cheerful heart is good medicine" (Prov. 17:22).

In your journal, jot down the "fun" you see each day. Look for bumper stickers, signs, commercials on TV, or bits of conversations from others at work or at the store that amuse you. Capture the humor in your world and don't be afraid to laugh.

Prayer

Teach me to laugh more, to sing more, to dance more as I think of what You have done in my life. May I see You as the Giver of laughter and may that endear You to me more. Amen.

When You Walk

Find things on your walk today that make you smile. Will you let yourself laugh?

Eighteen

FINDING TRACES OF BEAUTY

I lift up my eyes to the mountains—
where does my help come from?

—PSALM 121:1

In Japan's cities, space is tight. Yet even in the midst of tall office buildings, you can find a small token of beauty—a bonsai or rock garden. What a contrast it always was to me as a child growing up in Osaka to have large buildings towering over me and then to see a simple flower arrangement in a shop window or a lone cherry tree by a train station.

Look for the beauty in your neighborhood. I have one road I call my favorite cul-de-sac because of the garden by one house's mailbox. Each spring there are petunias and

Gerbera daisies. In the winter, a small pine is adorned by the homeowners in tiny Christmas baubles.

Sometimes seeing the same sights each day is not enough. The answer to my routine or confinement is a road trip. Plan one. It doesn't have to be extensive, just enough to get away from your daily habitat. Take your camera and a note pad or journal with you. Find a park, a mountain range, a forest, or a lake. Spend time being in nature, observing the surroundings. Note the shape of a cloud, the angle of a rocky peak, a duck in the water. Listen. Close your eyes and breathe in and out for few moments. Open your eyes and take time to see. Capture some of the sights with your camera. Be inspired! Write a few adjectives to describe what you see, how you feel. Let a poem or a psalm come from your heart.

Thank God for His creation. And that includes thanking God for you!

Reflections to Ponder

Frame one of the pictures you took on a recent road trip. Keep it in a place where you can be reminded of how valuable spending time in God's splendor is.

Sitting by my computer is a picture of the ocean I took. When I look at the foamy waves, I feel alive, peaceful, and blessed. Which words describe how you feel when you gaze at your photo?

Prayer

Before you pray, think about your posture. Yes, you read that right. The writer of Psalm 121 lifts up his eyes to the mountain as he seeks the source of his help. Many of us have been taught to kneel and fold our hands when we pray. In Psalm 134:2, the reference is, "Lift up your hands in the sanctuary and praise the LORD." In Deuteronomy 9:18, Moses claimed he "fell prostrate before the LORD for forty days and forty nights," praying for his rebellious people. As you pray, think of your body. How can you change your posture and your heart when you pray?

Dear God, Creator of nature, let me bask in the awe of the mountains, the flowers, the birds, and the trees. Let me enjoy the time spent walking in Your vast and unique creation.

May I find beauty in my work this week, in my relationships with my children, with my spouse, with my parents, and with my coworkers. May I seek to always look for the beauty around me. Amen.

When You Walk

Plan a walk in your local park. Take a souvenir home with you—a leaf, a blade of grass, a pinecone. Let this token remind you of how God delights in His creation and in you.

SECTION THREE

Sustained to Encourage

Nineteen

BEING REACHED

*Therefore confess your sins to each other and pray
for each other so that you may be healed. The prayer
of a righteous person is powerful and effective.*

—JAMES 5:16

There are two reasons I keep to myself when I'm going through a season of struggle. First, I don't want to burden others with my problems when I know they have their own crosses to bear. Second, I'm afraid I might be judged.

I suppose we live much of our lives wondering what others think of us. We feel we need to please others. Teasingly, I tell my kids that most people are too caught up in themselves to give them much thought. "So, don't worry," I conclude. "No one is noticing that your shorts have a tiny rip in the seam or that your nose is sunburned."

When it comes to being reached in our times of distress, you have to realize that your need to unload on loving ears and hearts is essential for your health. If you can find one person to share your situation with, consider yourself blessed. In fact, it is probably best to keep your woes to that one person. Even though I have taken a while to unleash my burdens to someone else, the times that I have dismissed my fears and gone ahead with asking for a listening ear have proven to be wonderful and freeing.

Allow others to come along beside you and be a friend. Having the trust to share our burden with someone is scriptural. We need the prayers, support, and love of others, especially during our seasons of turmoil.

A nugget of truth is that often, as we share, others are encouraged by what they learn from our struggles. Inviting someone to walk with you on your journey offers that person the opportunity to see God at work as he or she prays for you and supports you.

 Reflections to Ponder

What might keep you from sharing with others about your situation and need for prayer? What makes you want to share with others?

Prayer

Lord, when I am lonely, provide me with listening ears. When I am unable to explain how I feel, give me words. May I feel Your companionship today.

When You Walk

Commit these verses penned by Paul in 2 Corinthians 12:9–10 to memory as you walk today:

> *"My grace is sufficient for you, for my power is made perfect in weakness." Therefore, I will boast all the more gladly about my weaknesses, so that Christ's power may rest on me. That is why, for Christ's sake, I delight in weaknesses, in insults, in hardships, in persecutions, in difficulties. For when I am weak, then I am strong.*

Twenty

GIVER OF
COMFORT

*Blessed are those who mourn,
for they will be comforted.*
—MATTHEW 5:4

At those times when we feel useless, if we make ourselves useful we can find a sense of fulfillment.
Doing for others, whether it be making a meal for someone who has just had surgery or taking care of a pet while
friends are away, can add to our own comfort as well as
that of those we care for.

There are times when it feels right to stand beside a
needy friend and offer consolation. There are other times
when we balk at the task because of our own emotions and
feelings of inadequacy. When I found out that my friend

Cres, whom I had not seen in years, was hospitalized and that her body was shutting down because of sepsis, sorrow hit my core. But visiting her? Could I do that? Fifteen years ago my Daniel had suffered an infection and went into sepsis right before his death. Cres, my friends said, was dying. Daniel had died. "I don't do hospitals," I wrote to the email group of Cres's friends. I just couldn't.

Cres's mom arrived from Swaziland, and, as I pictured this stranger having to see her baby incubated, I wanted to hug her and bestow my empathy to her. Yet could I head over to the hospital? *God, if I go, will you prepare the path for me?* As I tried to concentrate on my writing deadline, my mind was pulled toward going to see Cres. Unable to ignore the impulse one afternoon, I cut my writing time at the library short, and without telling anyone, made my way toward Duke Medical Center. I drove, determined to get into the parking deck, because I knew once I got there I wouldn't have the option of turning back.

After meeting her brother and sister, I was given a paper robe and plastic gloves to wear into her ICU room. A silent Cres lay with the buzzing machines surrounding her, and to her right sat her mother on a chair, a little woman with a balled up tissue. A little woman with pain the size of Montana. How I knew that agony! After talking to a coma-induced Cres, stroking her arm and praying for her, I looked over at her mother. Before leaving, I had to hug this woman. As she stood up to meet me, we embraced. Her arms grew tight around me; I didn't want to let her go.

When I got to the hospital parking deck, I toppled into my Jeep and let those tears out. I cried for Cres's family, for the unfairness of illness, and yes, I sobbed because, even after all these years, I still miss my son.

Did I offer comfort? From my perspective I knew Cres's mom needed tissues, and the hospital staff supplied that for her. I also knew she needed a hug, and I hope she felt the connection of mother-to-mother grieving. But most of all, I felt I had gone to the hospital out of obedience to God, allowing Him to care for me as I showed compassion for others.

Reflections to Ponder

When you hear bad news, and often news does come in waves, take time to sit down. Too often we feel the need to run around or continue doing what we were doing at the time the phone rang. Sit. Be aware of your breathing. After praying for the person who has been hospitalized or for the coworker who was just laid off, tell yourself some positive truths. Focus on God, who reigns in the midst of chaos. He is near, He cares, He hears. And although it might be a common reaction, don't panic.

Who needs your comfort today?

Prayer

Dear God, don't let the empathy that you have cultivated in me ever be far from my reach. Let me be a respite of solace for the wounded. May I desire to give back as I have been given to.

In the name of the Creator of comfort, amen.

When You Walk

Think of Job and his aggravation after his devastation. How do we comfort so that those we have come to help don't belt out these words as Job did at his so-called comforters:

> *"I have heard many things like these;*
> *you are miserable comforters, all of you!*
> *Will your long-winded speeches never end?*
> *What ails you that you keep on arguing?"*
> (Job 16:2–3)

Think about how you can use your circumstances and what you have learned through them to be springboards of comfort for others.

Twenty-one

SERVICE TO OTHERS

The generous will prosper;
those who refresh others will themselves be refreshed.
—PROVERBS 11:25 NLT

When my friend Martha's son died suddenly, she was crushed with anguish. Wondering how she'd get through the upcoming holidays, she feared her first Christmas without her son. How would she survive the festivities when her son's absence would loom through every crevice of her house and heart? When the opportunity to help at a soup kitchen opened up for her, she took it. Christmas was spent preparing a meal for the lonely, the homeless, the needy. This was a lifeline for her. As she saw the crowd of people gather for the meal she'd helped prepare, she thought of how giving her son had been. What an honor to be able to reach others in his memory. Martha and others brought refreshment to a host of hungry people that day.

According to Merriam-Webster's online dictionary, the word *refresh* means to restore strength and animation to, to revive.

Even in our sorrow, it helps to look beyond our pain and know that ministering to others is possible. In fact, by doing so, we often find fulfillment. Through serving others, we look outside of our own pain and past ourselves.

Reflections to Ponder

Can I be the answer to someone's prayer today? Who around me needs my listening ear, my gift of a cup of coffee or tea, my undivided attention? Who can I refresh?

Prayer

Heavenly Father, let me think of others who have less than I do. Let me focus on those around me who cry out in pain. Use me to alleviate some of the suffering others have. I am weak, but with Your grace and strength, I can be used by You. Amen.

When You Walk

Thank God for His respite in your life.

Thank God for mentors.

Thank God for friends.

Thank God for family.

Thank God for struggles that cause you to know He is power and strength in a frail world.

Thank God that you are an overcomer!

Bask in the Resurrection story and what it means for you.

Twenty-two

SIMPLE ACTIONS BRING SUNLIGHT

The LORD is gracious and righteous;
our God is full of compassion.
—PSALM 116:5

Fondly, I recall a man who brought me a cup of coffee (mind you, hospital coffee, not Starbucks) each morning as I entered the clinic with my kids for my four-year-old Daniel's radiation treatment. I'd just gotten a child off to first grade, had a toddler in the stroller, bald-headed Daniel walking next to me, and was pregnant—we must have looked a sight. This stranger presented me with a cup of coffee every morning for two weeks. Coffee from a Styrofoam cup has never tasted as good as it did back on those chilly and fatigued mornings. The man was uniformed, an employee of the hospital, although I never knew exactly what his position was. That really didn't matter. Fifteen years later, I am still warmed by his kindness.

What we do for one another does make a difference, and is remembered. Can we dare to be people of compassion and seek those who might benefit from our kindness? Even when we are feeling the anguish from some area of our own lives, can we take that step out of ourselves and offer kindness to another?

❧ Reflections to Ponder

When was the last time you reached out to show an act of compassion? How did you feel afterwards? Do you believe that God sees all you do? How is God compassionate toward you?

Prayer

Lord, help me to be aware that I can seek to serve by offering kindness, however small, to those around me. Open my heart to becoming sensitive to what I can do to make a positive difference in the lives of others.

❧ When You Walk

Think of five ways you can serve a neighbor, a family member, or a coworker this week. What is the most extravagant thing you could do for someone? What is the simplest? Note the small flower, the larger trees. Is one more important or beautiful than the other to you?

Twenty-three

ESPECIALLY FOR PARENTS

May the God who gives endurance and
encouragement give you the same attitude of mind
toward each other that Christ Jesus had . . .
—ROMANS 15:5

There are times when the woes we hold in our hearts for our precious children are too large or personal to share with another. We keep our thoughts to ourselves. Perhaps we are afraid that we might be judged if we admit that our child has mental issues, or has been in trouble with the law. We don't want to fail or be labeled by others as unsuccessful. We want to be in control, all the while knowing that, from the moment the umbilical cord was cut, our child has been moving towards independence.

As a parent of a teen, you might think back to when your son was a mass of curls with a sweet smile, clinging to his daddy. How far he has come from that season of his life! Now he's got traffic violations and a sarcastic attitude. Some days you'd like to run from him because he's causing you stress and you aren't sure what to do anymore.

As we struggle to be steady and loving to our children even when we don't necessarily feel up to it or equipped for the task, we turn to God the Father. Help! We might grow impatient and frustrated at God. You gave him to me, why can't You make him listen (obey, love, like, respect, act kind) to me? When my eldest was ready for college, I (a single mom at the time) said, "Great, now East Carolina University can have her. Let the professors and advisors and peers help her become the person she's to be. For her stage in life right now, I've exhausted all my resources here at home."

I wanted my daughter to grow up and hoped the next step for her—obtaining a degree in college—would help. She still had miles to go then, as she hadn't fully put aside her unruly behavior from high school. My patience was tested many nights.

Parenting isn't for wimps. There are times when I've been faced with my own difficult parenting season and asked, "Now, where is the parent?" Oh . . . it's me. Sigh. I was hoping Mrs. Brady of the *Brady Bunch* or her maid, that other Alice, would step in and do this work for me.

Often, if we don't want to publicize among our church or friends what our precious darling is up to, it's good to find just one person we can confide in. This person could be a parent of a child who is in a situation similar to yours. The beauty of being able to pray for another exasperated parent's child is a blessing. Commit yourself to praying daily for the parents of this particular son or daughter as well as for their child. Update prayer requests through phone calls or email messages with the other parent.

A tip I have found useful is to pretend I'm in a play. I'm an actress and my desire is to play my part well. The master director is God. He casts the roles. I have my lines and give them and then have to listen to the lines of others who join me on stage. I can't say the other actors' lines or fill in for their part; I can only play mine. This tip helps me cope, making me quite aware that I am not the director; I am not the one in control. I have been asked to play only a part.

Reflections to Ponder

How can you love your child today? Can you see him or her as whole, as healed, even if the circumstances are bleak now?

Prayer

Lord, You are aware of my silent woes. You hear my cries for each child. Encourage me today. Show me how to walk in Your hope. Most of all, remind me of just how much You love my child. Amen.

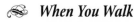 ### *When You Walk*

As you walk, say the names of your children and those of your friends' children. Lift each name before God. Ask God to help you and other parents as you all partake with Him of one of life's most challenging and rewarding tasks—being a mother, father, stepparent, guardian, or grandparent—to a child who is difficult.

Twenty-four

NO PERFECT LIFE

A heart at peace gives life to the body,
but envy rots the bones.
—PROVERBS 14:30

We look at others and wonder why they never seem to have heartaches. Their marriages are intact; their children are all healthy. They've got good teeth, bosses who value them, gardens filled with flowers, loving friends, and savings in the bank. Life seems peaceful and easy for them.

We let our minds go from noticing how right their lives seem to wanting what they have. We peer over that proverbial fence and watch. Our hearts flood with wanting. Envy and jealously take root and slowly, like a poison, they steal from our joy and the growth we have made.

If we only see those whom we "think" have it all together, then we will feel like the outcast. However, when we expand our vision we realize that there are many who are in dire straits. Not everyone is living the good life. Not everyone has everything in order. Others are suffering. Many of them are learning to cope well with unplanned situations that cause stress and strife. If we are so focused on how others might have it better, we neglect their cries when they are in need. And they will be in need, because the truth is there is no perfect life.

Open up! Listen! Look! Get out of your small consuming greed and envy focus. Don't let it take away from who you are—a precious treasure. Fill your mind with life-giving verses. Expand on what you can become as a child of God. God is working through you and He will equip you to do wonderful things for others. When we reach out to others, we take the limelight off of ourselves. In doing so, we lessen the focus on self and turn to God through asking, "How can I help? What can I do? What does my friend need? How can I meet that need? Show me, Lord."

What if we walk alongside someone else who is in sorrow today? "Grief shared is grief divided; joy shared is joy multiplied." What happens when we use our compassion to bless others?

❧ *Reflections to Ponder*

Seek out someone who is going through a struggle now. Walk along beside them to listen, to share, and to lift concerns up to God together.

Prayer

Show me how to be:
A cheerful giver
An encourager
A seeker of truth
A lover of loving well
A good listener
One who doesn't rain on other people's parades
One who asks about others
One who keeps accounts of the rights, not of other people's wrongs

Nudge me when I start to let my mind trail down the path of envy, jealousy, and greed. Show me how to fill my mind instead with verses of affirmation about who You are and how much You love me. Amen.

When You Walk

Recall how you have been helped by others. What have others done for you in your time of need? How can you offer compassion and hope in your church, community, and family?

SECTION FOUR

Sustained to Thrive

Twenty-five

CELEBRATE LIFE

Your love, LORD, reaches to the heavens,
your faithfulness to the skies.

—PSALM 36:5

As he listened to the songs of birds, my dad once said that he bet they were singing, "Praise God!" As part of creation, I often want to join nature in praising God. Yet, how often do I do it? Much of the time, I feel my mind is on what I don't have instead of what I do. The Bible speaks of the sacrifice of praise and of pleasing God by rejoicing in Him. Sometimes I have a hard time believing that anything I can do is pleasing to God.

When we feel fractious or discombobulated about our daily lives, when we are overwhelmed with sorrow or agony due to our circumstances, it's hard to praise. It's hard to find anything positive. Yet, what a difference it makes when we can find at least one nugget of truth or one object to rejoice about. It might only be the bloom of a single rose, the fragrance of our favorite detergent (I love the mountain fresh aroma), or a cup of hot tea.

Count each day as a gift. These are words that are now almost a cliché because they are used together so often. But when we are faced with the sudden death of a loved one or someone in our community or church, we realize these words are significant. Life can change in an instant. Questions hit us: What really matters? What is really important?

As we seek God's face each day, we can learn to incorporate celebration into our lives. Viewing life as a gift and believing that it can be good again is vital. We might feel discouraged because of the situation we're in, but gradually, we can see the sun through the clouds.

Reflections to Ponder

Start the day with a single praise to God. What can you praise Him for? It might just be that you were able to get out of bed or that you have clean clothes to wear.

Come up with three things you are thankful for. These can be simple things, but as long as you view them as blessings, that's what matters. Write these three things down in a notebook or journal. Expand on why you are thankful for them.

> *Prayer*
> Dear Lord, may I choose to be disciplined to seek the good, the excellent, the praiseworthy in this day. Help me to lift my head and my arms up so that my spirit may be lifted.

⮂ *When You Walk*

Carry a notepad or recording device with you on your walk today so that you can jot down or record ideas that come to you about ways to celebrate life. These can be simple things, such as inviting a friend over for coffee, or more involved, like redecorating a room in your home. Think of things that give you joy.

Paint a picture, grow an herb garden, take a class and learn something new. There are dozens of possibilities to add some zest to your life as you find ways to celebrate who you are.

Twenty-six

GOD OF MYSTERY

"For my thoughts are not your thoughts,
neither are your ways my ways,"
declares the LORD.

—ISAIAH 55:8

I grew up on Nancy Drew and Agatha Christie mysteries. Mysteries entice us to try to figure out who committed the crime before the detective knows. While that's fun, seldom do we want our lives to be the mystery. We want answers. Now.

When my son died, I wanted to know why. I will always wonder why he didn't get to live. I doubted the effectiveness of prayer for a long time after his last breath, because not only had he prayed for his healing, but so had I, his father, his grandparents, and countless people around the globe. There are other things I also don't understand about why things in life happen the way they do.

God doesn't have to tell us why He allows what He does. He's God. He never promised that He would explain all things to us. He wants us to trust that He holds the answers, just as He holds our lives. I wish that God would fill me in; but then, when I stand under the multitude of stars, I realize just how small I am. Of course, He doesn't have to share His ideas with me. Who am I? Even so, I often bellow out at Him, expecting Him to tell me what He's doing. Then, I'll conclude that even on a good day, my tiny mind probably couldn't handle His thoughts anyway.

You might be like I was. When Daniel died, I had to go over all the details leading up to his passing. Metaphorically, I was like a stomper of grapes; over and over my feet crushed them out of their skins into liquid. I left no grape unsmashed. I wondered why things ended the way they did with Daniel's life and wrestled with many issues. I banged on Heaven's door, so to speak, begging for God to show me why my four-year-old had to die. Did I get the answers as to why Daniel died? Eventually, I placed my questions in a box, sealed it, and stored the box in the attic of my mind. It was unnecessary for me to continue asking. Yet, since I am a wrestler by nature, I needed to ask in order for me to heal. Now there is no need to open the box and take out the mysteries and look them over. Time has passed and I have moved beyond those struggles.

I ask God to wipe my frustration away and to let me know I can keep going in spite of having no answers. I can keep looking up, even though I know that He does not always heal. He does not always spare the lives of loved ones. On some days that scares me. Why wouldn't a perfect God want an infant with a heart condition to be healed and live?

If we view ourselves as children—loved and cared for—does that make it easier to trust Him as the One who desires our trust, who longs for us to come to Him and exercise our little faith even in the midst of despair?

What a relief it is to stop trying to figure God out and to, instead, deepen our trust in Him so much so that we truly believe with a childlike faith.

☙ *Reflections to Ponder*

Some are not interested in walking with God. From youth on, they have an idea of God that is, at best, filled with partial truths. Their concept of God might be that of a stoic controller who rains on everyone's parades, or a jolly Santa-type dishing out gifts. Many haven't bothered to get to know the true and living God, the Father of Jesus Christ, a man who was ridiculed, a friend to the lonely, a healer of broken hearts.

Have some of the things you've been told about life as a Christ-follower been found to be mistruths?

The God of the Bible is a God of mystery. Can you accept not knowing the whys and hows of your life? Can you trust a God you might not always understand? Do you have a "mystery file," a page in your journal where you store those things that have happened that you have no answer for?

Prayer

Lord, I wrestle. I don't understand. Help me as I grapple with the things I don't comprehend. May I lean on You so much that my trust and love for You grows.

When You Walk

As you walk, lift up your face to the sun. Note the sway of the tree limbs. Feel your heart beating. Take a deep breath. Be aware of the many ways God has orchestrated nature and all living things, including you. Could you create a tree, a flower, an insect? No, that is not your place. Let the God of mysterious creations fill your veins with the assurance that He is God.

Twenty-seven

GOD OF HISTORY

. . . to him who divided the Red Sea asunder
his love endures forever.
—PSALM 136:13

ewish tradition recalls the mighty acts of God throughout history. The stories of God's faithfulness were passed down from generation to generation, a reminder that God kept His covenant with Abraham, Isaac, and Jacob.

Looking at a God who has worked throughout history helps us to know Him better today. He cared about His people even though they complained and sinned. His love endured then and it still does today.

The Old Testament stresses the keeping of His end of the covenant again and again:

But it was because the LORD loved you and kept the oath he swore to your ancestors that he brought you out with a mighty hand and redeemed you from the land of slavery, from the power of Pharaoh king of Egypt. Know therefore that the LORD your God is God; he is the faithful God, keeping his covenant of love to a thousand generations of those who love him and keep his commandments. (Deut. 7:8–9)

As we look back and see how God worked in history, can we find assurance for how He will work in the future?

Reflections to Ponder

Read Psalm 77 aloud. Note how the psalm begins with a cry and how, in verse 11, the writer of it ponders God's "miracles of long ago." Think of your own relationship with God. Write a timeline of significant events in your life. Think of times you were in despair or turmoil. How did you pray? What did you receive?

Read Hebrews 11, often called the Hall of Fame of Faith. Make a list of the names of the men and women mentioned. What do you know about their stories of faith? Memorize verse 1: "Now faith is being sure of what we hope for and certain of what we do not see."

How do you live according to this verse?

Prayer

As we read about some of our favorite Bible characters, their stories resonate with us. We see how

---

you responded, Lord, and we are reminded of your holiness, your power, and your desire to be obeyed. Because of Jesus Christ, we are grafted into your family as your children. May we stand firm in our promise to live as loving children, faithful to your calling in our lives. Amen.

 ## When You Walk

Think of the family members in your life, present and past, who have taught you about God. What turmoil and hardships have they faced? How did they overcome?

Twenty-eight

GRATITUDE!

Let the message of Christ dwell among you richly as you teach and admonish one another with all wisdom through psalms, hymns, and songs from the Spirit, singing to God with gratitude in your hearts.
—COLOSSIANS 3:16

When things go well for me, how easy it is to think that I am being blessed because of something I've done. In reality, it has nothing to do with my faithfulness or goodness. My blessings are all because of a God who freely gives. When we think we receive because of something we've done, the focus is then on us, on our power, on our charm, instead of on God's consistent nature.

In spite of our sinful nature or lack of trust, God still provides us with gifts. When we ponder all He has done for us, we are amazed. We move forward in this gratitude, rejoicing that He is our God and we are His people.

It is common for people to stand and ask for prayer during a hardship. How encouraging it is when someone stands to share gratitude for what God has provided.

✍ *Reflections to Ponder*

List your blessings—the things you are grateful for, the people who are in your life, the experiences you have enjoyed, the hobbies that bring you comfort.

Keep a running list. Keep it by your bedside and add to it each day.

Look to Psalm 136 and read the first twenty verses aloud. Then try creating your own psalm with this pattern, filling in your own lines. Keep the refrain: His love endures forever.

> Give thanks to the LORD, for he is good.
> *His love endures forever.*
> Give thanks to the God of gods.
> *His love endures forever.*
> Give thanks to the Lord of lords:
> *His love endures forever.*
>
> to him who alone does great wonders,
> *His love endures forever.*
> who by his understanding made the heavens,
> *His love endures forever.* (Ps. 136:1–5)

We tend to add only the obviously positive blessings to our gratitude lists; but, sometimes, when we look back on our lives, we realize we would not have experienced growth if it weren't for the tough times. While the rocky paths are never to our choosing or liking, the attributes of God we experience during them are positives. And, by learning more of the nature of God, we yearn to become more like Him. Perseverance, humility, compassion, long suffering, and mercy have places on our gratitude lists!

Prayer

Open my eyes to the ways I am blessed. Teach me how to reach out to others and find ways to bless them.

 ### When You Walk

Think of someone to send a card to. Either purchase or make a card, pen a short note, and send it to someone after your walk.

Twenty-nine

GRIEF AS A GIFT

I will be glad and rejoice in your love,
for you saw my affliction
and knew the anguish of my soul.

—PSALM 31:7

My husband and I walked out our front door one evening to see a fire truck, an ambulance, and a police car parked outside my neighbor Claudia's home. Quickly we learned that, just minutes before, my neighbor had died, another neighbor by her side.

The situation was sad. But a year later, I'm not missing Claudia every day. My son, on the other hand, I miss profusely. His loss made a hole in my heart. His loss is felt even fifteen years later because of the love I had and continue to have for him.

We grieve because we love. Those who were not as close to us do not hold a grip on our hearts when they pass on. This grief can consume us, bury us, make us think we're going crazy—especially during the early years of longing for our loved one.

As we adapt and adjust to the holes in our hearts, can we view grief as a gift? Not the wallowing in the mud kind, but rather, a healthy good grief—a grief that is formed from love, not pity or self-destruction.

One of the gifts of grief for me is the realization of how short our lives here really are. It is often in death that we evaluate life. We hold it up before us and think, if I were to die today, what would my legacy be? What have I done that is memorable? Have I been generous with my love or tight fisted? Have I shared my resources, my time?

Evangelist Robert Schuller says, "Our grief always brings a gift. It's the gift of greater sensitivity and compassion for others. We learn to rise above our own grief by reaching out and lessening the grief of others" (34).

Can you rise above your grief and let your compassion be used as a gift to others? Can you walk alongside someone who is going through a loss similar to yours? What can you offer that person?

Genuine sorrow spills from our own hearts like a mountain waterfall and meets in the river below with the sorrow of others. While no situation of grief and loss is identical, there is enough commonality in mourning that swirls us together, binding us, often so much so that no words of explanation are needed.

The first time I saw my friend after her husband of nearly fifty years died, all I could do was hug her. In that tearful embrace, we were swirled together in the unity of both sharing what it is like to lose a beloved one to death. She was a new widow and I was a bereaved mother; our losses different, but also woven with similarities.

✑ *Reflections to Ponder*

If you were to die today, what do you think the reactions of others would be?

What would you like written on your gravestone? What charity or foundation would you want people to contribute to in your honor? What are ten things you would want to be remembered for?

Prayer

Lord, as important as I might think I am, I am not immortal. I am but a mist that appears for a little while and then vanishes. My days are numbered on this earth. May I use them well as I learn to adapt to my grief and deal with the challenges I am faced with.

✑ *When You Walk*

As you set out on you walk, rejoice in the lives that have gone on before you. Give thanks to God for the gift of Jesus Christ.

Thirty

ASKING FOR WISDOM AND COURAGE

If any of you lacks wisdom, you should ask God, who gives generously to all without finding fault, and it will be given to you. But when you ask, you must believe and not doubt, because the one who doubts is like a wave of the sea, blown and tossed by the wind.

—JAMES 1:5–6

I love to ask for wisdom. Perhaps it's because I have so little of my own. Clearly, to travel on these rocky paths of life, I need constant help in knowing what I need to do in the midst of my confusion. James makes asking easy. Plus, the verses from chapter 1 come with a sweet promise, a promise that you will get what you ask for—blessed wisdom.

In *The Message*, James 1:5–6 reads:

> *If you don't know what you're doing, pray to the Father. He loves to help. You'll get his help, and won't be condescended to when you ask for it. Ask boldly, believingly, without a second thought. People who "worry their prayers" are like wind-whipped waves. Don't think you're going to get anything from the Master that way, adrift at sea, keeping all your options open.*

After *boldly* asking for wisdom, ask for understanding as well. "Give me understanding that I may live," writes the psalmist in Psalm 119:144. The next verse shows his desperation, "I call with all my heart; answer me, LORD, and I will obey your decrees."

Many times I'm in the throes of some argument with my spouse or children and I realize I'm faltering. Have I asked for God's wisdom in the situation? Have I cried out with my whole heart for understanding? Do I ask with the certainty that God will supply me with the wisdom? Only He knows that troubles I've seen; only He knows just what I need at any given moment.

Reflections to Ponder

How do I treasure what God commands? How can I learn to yearn for wisdom and courage, instead of material things?

Prayer

God, give us grace to accept with serenity
the things that cannot be changed,
Courage to change the things
which should be changed,
and the Wisdom to distinguish
the one from the other.

(Original prayer by Reinhold Niebuhr, quoted in his daughter
Elizabeth Sifton's book, *The Serenity Prayer: Faith and Politics
in Times of Peace and War*, 277.)

When You Walk

Think of the joys and benefits that come with walking.

Think about the discipline it takes to commit to walking each day. When you walk on uphill trails, endurance comes into play. How do you keep going (especially when you are nearly out of breath)? I find it helps to focus on something pleasant to take my mind off how far I have to go to reach my goal (the end of the trail).

What are some disciplines you use in your spiritual life? How does practicing these disciplines benefit you?

Thirty-one

WORSHIP IN THE WILDERNESS

Then say to him, "The LORD, the God of the Hebrews,
has sent me to say to you: Let my people go,
so that they may worship me in the wilderness."

—EXODUS 7:16

We may feel we're in a wilderness, a season of uncertainty. This season is comfortable to say the least, and we wish we could be magically pulled out of it. We have no idea how long this wilderness will last—this unemployment, this rebellious child, this debilitating illness, this longing to be with the one who has died. We wonder if things can get worse. We moan, we complain, we forget to count our blessings.

Suddenly we are reminded of someone else and are able to take our eyes off of our own problems. Others are struggling, too. We open our Bible and read of the Israelites as they journeyed through the wilderness. Far from home, they longed for what was familiar. They were led with a cloud by day and fire by night. Mealtimes consisted of manna, a type of bread from Heaven that God provided. They grumbled. They wanted things to be different. Yet some of them trusted in spite of the sand between their toes, and thus, were able to sing. But we know that they were tempted to follow other gods, images they could mold and touch. Even so, God did not abandon them.

Paul says that he learned to be content in every circumstance. His ability to be content has been a prayer of mine for dozens of years. I'd like to be content because I have God with me and because God is enough. I know that in Him lies all I need to sustain me. Yet, I want to touch more. I, too, am guilty of desiring a tangible image.

Reflections to Ponder

How has God sustained you in your wilderness? How do you worship Him? What helps you keep your head up, looking upward, believing that you can sing a new song, even in an unknown land?

Read these verses from Psalm 95:

Come, let us sing for joy to the LORD;
let us shout aloud to the Rock of
our salvation.

Let us come before him with thanksgiving
and extol him with music and song. (vv. 1–2)

Come, let us bow down in worship,
let us kneel before the LORD our Maker;
for he is our God
and we are the people of his pasture,
the flock under his care. (vv. 6–7)

And these verses from Joshua 24:

Now fear the LORD and serve him with all faith-
fulness. Throw away the gods your ancestors wor-
shiped beyond the Euphrates River and in Egypt,
and serve the LORD. But if serving the LORD seems
undesirable to you, then choose for yourselves this
day whom you will serve, whether the gods your
ancestors served beyond the Euphrates, or the gods
of the Amorites, in whose land you are living. But as
for me and my household, we will serve the LORD.
(vv. 14–15)

How does the act of worship banish worry?

Prayer

Forgive me, Lord, for being a worshiper of you
one day and a believer in the power of money, the
security of education, fame, or fashion the next.
How foolish I can be to think that these "golden

calves" are worth bowing to and trusting in? You,
alone, can sustain me. You, alone, are worthy of
being served.

When You Walk

With each step you take, let it be a step to stomp out the
worry in your mind.

Thirty-two

A NEW SONG

He put a new song in my mouth,
a hymn of praise to our God.
Many will see and fear the LORD
and put their trust in him.
—PSALM 40:3

We have the potential to view a new vision and to make new priorities. With all the growing we have done, we don't want to return to our old, poor habits of reacting and thinking. We want to use what we've learned from the pit of grief to become more like Christ. We yearn for a new song and He gives us one to sing.

True, at times, we might not feel like singing; but thankfully, our feelings are not all there is to our faith. Often, it is about trusting and believing in spite of whether we feel God or not. Thank God that He doesn't operate on feelings. How grateful I am that there won't come a day when God says, "I don't feel like listening to Alice today. She's been whining way too much this week." God hears me regardless of how much I whine. He is constant, unchanging, and forever attentive to our cries. Knowing that makes me want to sing a song unto Him.

Reflections to Ponder

Read Psalm 96.

What is your usual song? If it is one of complaint, how can you find a new song to sing? What do you need to do to write the words to a song of praise and hope?

Think about other psalms that talk about song and singing. Consider choosing one you can memorize to recite in your car or as you complete your tasks for the day.

Listen to music that inspires you. As you listen, spend time writing freely what is in your heart. Later, create your own psalm of praise. If your heart is heavy, start your psalm with lament and see if it can end with the assurances God gives.

Prayer

Praise you, Lord. Let the praises from my mouth be sweet to Your ear. For the times I find it hard to see the good, give me hope that one day I will sing.

When You Walk

Listen for the sounds in nature. How many birds and insect songs can you identify?

SECTION FIVE

Sustained to Hope

Thirty-three

WAIT WITH HOPE

The Sovereign LORD *is my strength;*
he makes my feet like the feet of a deer,
he enables me to tread on the heights.

—HABAKKUK 3:19

Much of life is spent waiting. I'm constantly reminded of this when we hit a particular red light on the drive to my son's workplace. That traffic light can cause us to wait for up to four minutes. Waiting can be spent in dread, in impatience, in joy, or in quiet solitude. We wait with joy for a birth, and with sorrow for a death. We wait in doubt when it seems God is silent, and we feel we have been waiting for much too long.

What if we trusted God in our waiting and used the time to let God's strength pour over us? What if we saw value in waiting? Does waiting produce a time of growth so that our legs are able to stretch up to higher platitudes?

Sarah waited years to conceive. By the time she was an old woman, she'd given up hope. Moses waited to lead his people out of slavery. Jacob worked for seven years as he waited for Rachel to become his wife. The magi waited for the star that announced the birth of a King. Jesus waited in the Garden of Gethsemane for His hour to approach.

Reflections to Ponder

What did John the Baptist do as waited for the birth of Jesus?

In the Garden of Gethsemane, Jesus waited for the time to come when He would be arrested. As He waited, He prayed for Himself, for His disciples, and for all believers (John 17).

Can you depend on God to supply what you need as you wait?

Prayer

. . . those who hope in the LORD
will renew their strength.
They will soar on wings like eagles;
they will run and not grow weary,
they will walk and not be faint. (Isa. 40:31)

Personalize these verses and speak them aloud:

I who hope in the Lord will renew my strength

I will soar on wings like eagles;
I will run and not grow weary,
I will walk and not be faint.
God, teach me how to wait with hope.
I rise before dawn and cry for help;
I have put my hope in your word. (Ps. 119:147)

When You Walk

Push yourself to walk a little further today. Walk an extra two blocks or an extra mile. As you go this extra distance, think of five times that you have waited on God in the past and how the wait resulted.

Thirty-four

WAITING AGAIN

Wait for the LORD;
be strong and take heart
and wait for the LORD.
—PSALM 27:14

We wait, again. . . . I chose to create two devotions on waiting to stress the point that waiting is prominent in our daily living.

As a teen, I felt I wasted time. Now, as an adult, I look back and wish that I'd put that time to use more wisely. I could have been writing wonderful novels, reading dynamic books, or finding the cure for cancer. Now, when I wait, I don't just fritter time away, counting the minutes and hours away. I let waiting work for me; I wait with hope. I read Scripture pertaining to waiting on God as I seek His face. In Psalm 130, the psalmist waits more than those who watch for the morning. Like watchmen wait for the break of dawn, anticipating it, so does the writer of this psalm. He waits in the knowledge that God's mercy will arrive.

Although the waiting can be painful, he doesn't doubt. He is certain, not because of who he is, but because of who God is. Henri Nouwen, in *Finding My Way Home*, says, "To wait with openness and trust is an enormously radical attitude toward life" (101).

Can you be radical? Is God worth waiting for?

✎ *Reflections to Ponder*

Read Psalm 130. Slowly, read it aloud, pausing at each period.

> *Out of the depths I cry to you, O LORD,*
> > *O Lord, hear my voice.*
> *Let your ears be attentive*
> > *to my cry for mercy.*
>
> *If you, O LORD, kept a record of sins,*
> > *O Lord, who could stand?*
> *But with you there is forgiveness;*
> > *therefore you are feared.*
>
> *I wait for the LORD, my soul waits,*
> > *and in his word I put my hope.*
> *My soul waits for the Lord*
> > *more than watchmen wait for the morning,*
> > *more than watchmen wait for the morning.*
> *O Israel, put your hope in the LORD,*
> > *for with the LORD is unfailing love*

> *and with him is full redemption.*
> *He himself will redeem Israel*
> *from all their sins.*

What does this psalm say we are waiting for? Note how many times the verb *wait* is used. How about the word *hope*? Count the number of times *Lord* is used. When the word Lord is written as LORD (small capitals or all capitals), this shows that it has been translated from the Hebrew words Yahweh and Yah. Both Yahweh and Yah were God's personal names.

As you wait, look into your heart. Take time to examine your heart for bitterness or jealousy or for whatever sin you have trouble avoiding. Do any of these keep you from waiting with hope?

Prayer

Lord, may nothing come between You and me today. May I learn how to wait upon You with courage, with strength. May I live in the moment of waiting.

When You Walk

Pray as you walk, asking God to remind you of the things you have waited for and what happened when the time of waiting for them was up. Think about God's promises and spend time memorizing a few of them.

Thirty-five

GROWTH CHARTS

I waited patiently for the LORD;
he turned to me and heard my cry.
—PSALM 40:1

I love it when I'm faced with a challenge and react
to it in a more God-loving fashion than I did when
faced with a similar situation years ago. I love seeing how
far I've come in my walk with God. This is progress at its
best.

The disciples grew as they got to know Jesus and
learned from Him. Think of how they started out and the
concerns they held. Some left their nets to follow Him;
but as they walked with Him, ate with Him, and saw Him
perform supernatural tasks, they still questioned whether
He was the Messiah. When Jesus was led to the cross, they
feared for their own lives. After Jesus' victory over death,

they were able to see and so believed even more. Thomas knew Jesus was his Lord and God after seeing the nail prints in His hands and the spear hole in His side (John 20). Jesus' response to Thomas is a line meant for those of us who weren't around during that era. He said, "'Because you have seen me, you have believed; blessed are those who have not seen and yet have believed'" (John 20:29).

Growing up means change. Where we once doubted, we now see. Experience has opened our eyes. We have experienced God's grace, forgiveness, love, and power; and so, when a new situation arises, we have this history with God to bank on. He was with us when our spouse left. He provided for us when we were let go from our place of employment. He sent comfort when we received the devastating diagnosis. He has been with us all along. He will continue to be with us so that we can live, even thrive. Although we have not seen Jesus in the flesh as the disciples did, we have been privileged to walk in His spirit each day.

✑ *Reflections to Ponder*

Spend some time with your journal. Write down some of the things you've learned and list the ways you have changed. Fill in these blanks:

I used to feel _____.
I once thought _____.
Now I think _____.
Now I believe _____.
One day I hope to _____.

Keep a "Giving It Over to God" calendar where you can see it each day. On this calendar (make sure it has large squares), place a mark or some emblem to signify a problem that you are handing over to God. You could write the letter "J" for jealousy on the square for today, meaning you are giving over to God your difficulty with the problem of being envious of your neighbor or friend. Or perhaps you will write the letter "F" because you need to give over your refusal to forgive, and now is the day to do that.

As you place these markings on your calendar, ask God to take your difficulty or your sin and teach you how to grow out of it, away from it, and toward His likeness. Like a baby, we have to be weaned from our dependency or patterns into healthier mature attitudes.

Prayer

Help my unbelief, dear God. Instruct me on how to depend on You.

 ### When You Walk

If you can, take a path you haven't been on yet. See where it leads you. Think about situations in your life where you almost didn't do something or go somewhere, but chose to take a chance. What would you have missed had you not taken the road less traveled?

Thirty-six

EVEN WHEN IT'S BLEAK

Though the fig tree does not bud
and there are no grapes on the vines,
though the olive crop fails
and the fields produce no food,
though there are no sheep in the pen
and no cattle in the stalls,
yet I will rejoice in the LORD,
I will be joyful in God my Savior.
—HABAKKUK 3:17–18

I tell my children that life is tough. It isn't easy being human. I'm not trying to take away their hope. Rather, I want them to know that troubles will come their way; and, instead of shunning those troubles, they need to look up to God for help. Life and troubles go together. It took me a long time to realize this. I think the desire to believe that I would be spared from sorrows stunted my early spiritual growth.

Jesus warned us, "In this world you will have trouble" (John 16:33). The fig tree will often be bare. But each time, hopefully, our trust in God deepens. We look back and see how He provided even when we were ready to call it quits.

I pondered the reason that we rejoice even when the fig tree doesn't bud and realized that being joyful in God serves a wonderful purpose. If we can focus on God, this takes our mind off of the circumstances that plague us. If we can keep our eyes on a God who changes not, who is constant even though our lives are whirlwinds of change, we are acting on the knowledge that we serve Someone worthy of praise. We let praise overtake our burden. Praise gets the front row seat. Our heavy turmoil gets seated in the back of the auditorium. Time and time again, God asks us to look to Him as our Refuge, to focus on His goodness in spite of our sorrow. Something about trusting in the midst of bleakness works to reiterate the worthiness of God to be praised. Even when things aren't as we want them to be. Even when the day is dark. Regardless.

While Jesus said in John 16:33 that we will have trouble, He also left us with a promise in that same verse: "But take heart! I have overcome the world." Our problems won't go with us into our new life in Heaven. But God will.

I challenge you to get to know God better than you know your troubles. Push aside all the jargon you might have grown up with—"Christianese"—certain phrases you've repeated that you aren't even sure how to explain to a nonbeliever. Read the Bible, perhaps pondering on one passage over and over so that you can fully grasp its meaning for you. Discover ways to express both God and faith in your own words.

✇ *Reflections to Ponder*

Can we trust that God is moving even when all seems impossible? When we have nothing to hang onto but God, when everything else seems at a loss, a mural of confusion, can we know that God is for us?

Prayer

Lord, I want to persevere. I want to be persistent as I serve You—believing that You are for me, that Your love for me is great, and that Your mercy and grace exceed my expectations.

✇ *When You Walk*

When there are days you don't feel like going on your daily walk, how do you motivate yourself? If someone asked you what to do to become motivated, what advice would you give?

Thirty-seven

PRACTICING CONTENTMENT

I am not saying this because I am in need,
for I have learned to be content
whatever the circumstances.
—PHILIPPIANS 4:11

If it were easy, there wouldn't be so much written about how to do it. Paul doesn't talk about the pursuit of happiness. He's focused on a higher accomplishment. Being content is the ability to be satisfied with what one has, whether it is a little or a lot. Once we have reached the ability to be content, we have reached a high goal. There is a peace that comes with being satisfied. It causes one to refrain from looking over one's shoulder at others, desiring what they have. By no means does the ability to be content mean that a life is trouble-free; rather, in spite of those pesky circumstances, the heart can say, "I am at rest."

How do we go about obtaining this goal? I think it comes from knowing and loving Jesus more. Those who have gone through turmoil often have a high level of contentment. They've experienced the worst fires and storms. They've seen God's provision, His grace, His mercy. These blessings are rooted in their core. They aren't rattled because they look back and see what God has done in their history. They trust He will again act. They sing, "It is well with my soul."

They also look for ways to be sustained along the way. Their answers may not come immediately; but as they wait, they know that God will give them His comfort, His love, His presence.

✎ *Reflections to Ponder*

Read Psalm 145. Take some time to write your own response to it.

Prayer

You are faithful to Your promises; You are loving toward all You have made. You uphold all those who fall, and lift up all who are bowed down. I thank you, Lord, for Your faithfulness to me.

✺ *When You Walk*

Commit this to memory as you walk:

> *The Lord sustains the humble. . . .* (Ps. 147:6)

Thirty-eight

WHEREVER YOU GO

I am with you and will watch over you wherever you go,
and I will bring you back to this land. I will not leave you
until I have done what I have promised you.
—GENESIS 28:15

here is nothing quite like being thrown into a country where you not only don't speak the language, but clearly look and act like a foreigner. So it was for me when I went to Costa Rica to study for six months during my junior year in college. Aware of how much I was at the mercy of my host family, I relied on them for advice. Since they spoke no English and my Spanish was only textbook style, I depended on God to come through for me.

I leaned on Him, drawing near to Him. He was near me as I adjusted to life in this tropical land, innocently butchered the language too many times, smiled often to cover my uncertainties, and, while alone in my bedroom, underlined all the passages about God being close.

My ignorance surfaced when, years later, I was employed with a Protestant church in Kobe, Japan, and had to leave the country in order to get a proper visa. I decided to make a trip to Malaysia, visit a friend, and apply for a work visa at the embassy there. The foolish part played in when I got to Kuala Lumpur right after Ramadan. This is a Muslim country, I thought. They'll never give me a visa to work in a Christian church in Japan. How I prayed that night!

The next day, I headed to the embassy with skepticism mixed with a host of Scripture verses about trusting God. On the bus, I silently prayed, *God, you gave me the desire to work in Japan; please take away the desire if I'm not going to legally be able to teach there.* I thought of all my plans to live and work in Kobe and wondered if they would never come to pass.

Once at the embassy, I submitted my documents through a tiny window and was told by the Muslim employee to come back the next day. I went sightseeing with my friend, ate some great Malaysian food, and tried to turn down the worry as I slept that night. When I returned to the embassy the next morning, I was presented with a three-year missionary visa—the best kind available.

O ye of little faith.

More important than my lack of faith was that God was with me, providing for me so that I could teach English and Bible at a church in Japan.

✍ *Reflections to Ponder*

Think of a time when God provided for you in a situation you thought was impossible.

Prayer

Thank you for my faith—a gift You have given to me.

✍ *When You Walk*

Pray for those who are overseas, away from home and family. Pray that they can sustain the difficulties they encounter. Pray for their faith to increase and flourish.

Thirty-nine

ETERNAL HOPE

Now we know that if the earthly tent we live in is
destroyed, we have a building from God, an eternal
house in heaven, not built by human hands.
—2 CORINTHIANS 5:1

While I am an advocate for tears and believe that we need to cry every so often to cleanse our bodies, I am not an advocate of the reasons for having to cry or for the puffy red eyes that follow. My son told me one night in the hospital that there is no crying in Heaven. I wonder how he knew this and why he chose to tell me; but since his death, this is one of the phrases I hear often as I remember his short and sweet life.

We look to Heaven, knowing that, as Christians, we have been promised more. Life on earth, with all its unfairness, is not all there is. As the song "Great Is Thy

Faithfulness" resounds, "strength for today and bright hope for tomorrow." We trust in a future with God where there will be no more weeping, no more sickness, no more sorrow. The child who has had to suffer all her life with cystic fibrosis will have healthy lungs (in her new body, of course), and the child who never walked will run through fields of daisies.

Regardless of how your life has been here on earth, no one can steal from you the hope that comes with trusting God for an eternity with Him.

🐚 *Reflections to Ponder*

What does the word *hope* mean to you? Do you clutch onto it like a life preserver? How do you value Jesus' death on the cross to provide that hope? What is eternal hope to you?

Prayer

Thank you, Lord, for saving my soul,
Thank you, Lord, for making me whole,
Thank you, Lord, for giving to me,
Thy great salvation, so rich and free. ("Thank You Lord")

🐚 *When You Walk*

Pray for those who have no hope.

Bring before God those you know who have rejected Him. Commit to praying for them by name.

Forty

WE ARE ALL
PILGRIMS HERE

*"Show me, LORD, my life's end
and the number of my days;
let me know how fleeting is my life."*
—PSALM 39:4

I can't imagine a book on how to wake up in the
morning not having a chapter on the promise of
eternity. When we bask in the truth that life is more than
what we see, that there is hope and real living outside
of this small existence on this deteriorating planet, our
hearts can soar. For the beauty is that we were created
to be more than this life on earth. And as we groan and
moan and are tempted to become weary at the injustices,
let's keep an eye toward the reward of what is to come.

We are only aliens here—only on a pilgrimage. Our days are limited. Hallelujah! We don't have to live in this chaos forever and ever. Our lives in this world are but a breath compared to our eternity with Jesus Christ in our other home, Heaven.

As an American missionary kid growing up in Japan, I was often perplexed. I knew Japan, loved the food and trains, went to school, had friends, ministered in my parents' church, and felt that Japan was my home. But I looked different from everyone else because I was five foot nine with blond hair, and children would remind me that I was *gaijin* (someone from the outside). In the United States, I blended in with my looks, but I felt out of place. I'd spent little time in the states, and much of the culture was strange to me. Just entering a grocery store overwhelmed me because of all the brands of breakfast cereal. I think, early on, I was conditioned to feel like a stranger, an outsider, a foreigner. From childhood, I wondered where I belonged.

For those of us who have had experiences that are not ordinary, we, too, can feel displaced in our own towns. But we are not meant to become comfortable here. We know that there is some place better than our earthly home—a space where we are accepted no matter what, a banquet table where we are called by name and not ridiculed for being different.

✍ *Reflections to Ponder*

How will you live today thinking about your real home? Does releasing your grasp on the things of this life bring you peace? Does it change your perspective?

> *Prayer*
>
> O soul, are you weary and troubled?
> No light in the darkness you see?
> There's light for a look at the Savior,
> And life more abundant and free!
>
> Turn your eyes upon Jesus,
> Look full in His wonderful face,
> And the things of earth will grow strangely dim,
> In the light of His glory and grace. ("Turn Your
> Eyes upon Jesus")

✍ *When You Walk*

Think of how God sustains you and what it means to be sustained. As you walk, think of how your heart is pumping blood; concentrate on your breathing, your pulse, the way your legs bend. What a privilege to be able to walk and talk freely to Jesus. What an honor to look forward to the gift of Heaven. One day, we will see Him face to face!

Resources

Bonhoeffer, Dietrich. *Life Together and Prayerbook of the Bible*. Minneapolis: Augsburg Fortress, 2004.

Claypool, John R. *Tracks of a Fellow Struggler*. New Orleans: Insight Press, 1974.

Lewis, C. S. *A Grief Observed*. New York: HarperOne, 1989.

Nouwen, Henri J. M. *Finding My Way Home*. New York: Crossroad, 2001.

Peterson, Eugene H. *A Year with the Psalms: 365 Meditations and Prayers*. Waco, Texas: Word Books, 1979.

———. *Praying with Paul: A Year of Daily Prayers and Reflections on the Words of Paul*. New York: Harper San Francisco, 1995.

Rupp, Joyce. *Praying our Goodbyes*. Notre Dame: Ave Maria Press, 1988.

Sifton, Elizabeth. *The Serenity Prayer: Faith and Politics in Times of Peace and War*. New York: W. W. Norton, 2005.

Zadra, Dan, and Marcia Woodard, comp. *Forever Remembered*. Seattle: Compendium, 1997.

What Helps You Get Up in the Morning?

"What helps me get up in the morning is the responsibility for keeping my son Daniel's memory alive." —Elizabeth Hendershot

"Knowing that my family needs to see my face and get a hug from me before they go to school or work. That alone helps me get up at 5:30 every morning." —Anne Paulson

"Choosing to believe that if yesterday held sorrow, today holds healing—however incremental; if yesterday was full of regrets, today I get to tear the wrapper off a whole new gift of grace." —Kit Tosello

"I leave my blinds up a few inches when I go to bed, just enough so that when I wake up I see the mountains first thing. Some mornings, birds are singing over a bright pink dawn; some mornings are heavy and gray. But the mountains remind me that my steadfast Father God is present again for me today." —Kit Tosello

"Since I have fibromyalgia, I slowly stretch my muscles while still in my warm bed before going vertical. My feet then get into arch-supported slippers, go downstairs to three doggies who need food and love. Then I eat a healthy breakfast and count out my million meds for the day." —Dr. L. B. Greer

"What helps me get up in the morning is being able to say, 'This is the day the Lord has made. I will be glad and rejoice in it' (Ps. 118:24). It helps to have a schedule: I go to an aerobics class each morning, and have a quiet time of study and prayer before I go—so I have to get out of bed and get busy!" —Katharine Parrish

"When there is pain and sorrow, the word that comes to mind is momentum. I see this as a GGG (God-Given Grace), since my mind and will are often not fully online or engaged at that time of day. The habit of service also: making coffee for our eighteen-year-old to grab in flight on exit, the gentle nudge to a daughter who'd rather sleep-in, beginning the chores which others rather not do. These things—though mundane—have a transcendently lasting, loving quality to them (I hope)." —Bob Mutter

"I keep a list of what I need to do each day. When my husband first died, I placed everything on it, including *eat breakfast, check the mail, watch the news on TV.* Having lists helped me start my day and gave me a sense of being productive."
—Jackie L.

"While it is still dark outside, I need to sit very quietly in my chair by the window and sip my coffee. No TV, no radio, just silence. At that time I am neither happy nor sad, I am simply me with no expectations for the day." —Debbie Hearne

"The fact that I have an 8–5, Monday through Friday job, the knowledge that a cup of coffee will soon be ready, and for the past six-and-a-half years knowing God is there to give me the strength and endurance I need to get through each day, even when I don't 'feel' like it."
—Robin Nixon

TIPS FOR WRITING THE HEARTACHE

1. Buy a journal; make sure to buy it because it's one you like, not just because it's on sale.
2. Spend some alone time with a pen and your journal.
3. Don't worry about grammar or penmanship.
4. Write freely.
5. Write honestly.
6. Write your struggles, your fears, your woes.
7. Write a psalm of lament.
8. Write a psalm of praise.
9. Capture quotes and Scripture that are meaningful to you.
10. Know that your journal will not judge you or ridicule you.
11. Write with the feeling that you will survive this.
12. Write a love letter.
13. Pen your memories.
14. Describe your favorite place.
15. Spend time reflecting on where you've been and where you're going.

16. Share your journal entries with a friend or choose not to share—the decision is up to you.
17. Write knowing that, through the act of writing from your loss and grief, you are writing for healing, health, and hope.

About the Author

In 1997, Alice J. Wisler's four-year-old son Daniel died after eight months of vigorous cancer treatments. In his memory, Alice founded Daniel's House Publications, a grief organization, to help other parents cope with death. Through this organization, she created "Writing the Heartache" workshops, geared to help others discover the benefits of writing from losses. Alice is the author of five novels (two Christy finalists), the most recent being *Still Life in Shadows*. She lives in Durham, NC, with her husband and children. Visit her *Writing the Heartache* blog at http://writingtheheartache.blogspot.com/, her *Broken Psalms* blog at http://www.danielshouseworkshop.blogspot.com/, and her Website at http://www.alicewisler.com.